GETTING TO SCALE

Getting to Scale

Growing Your Business
Without Selling Out

Jill Bamburg

BERRETT-KOEHLER PUBLISHERS, INC.
San Francisco

Berrett-Koehler Publishers, Inc.
235 Montgomery Street, Suite 650
San Francisco, CA 94104-2916
Tel: (415) 288-0260   Fax: (415) 362-2512   www.bkconnection.com

Ordering Information
Quantity sales. Special discounts are available on quantity purchases by nonprofit organizations, corporations, associations, and others. For details, contact the "Special Sales Department" at the Berrett-Koehler address above.
Individual sales. Berrett-Koehler publications are available through most bookstores. They can also be ordered directly from Berrett-Koehler: Tel: (800) 929-2929; Fax: (802) 864-7626; www.bkconnection.com
Orders for college textbook/course adoption use. Please contact Berrett-Koehler: Tel: (800) 929-2929; Fax: (802) 864-7626.
Orders by U.S. trade bookstores and wholesalers. Please contact Publishers Group West, 1700 Fourth Street, Berkeley, CA 94710. Tel: (510) 528-1444; Fax: (510) 528-3444.

Berrett-Koehler and the BK logo are registered trademarks of Berrett-Koehler Publishers, Inc.

Printed in the United States of America
Berrett-Koehler books are printed on long-lasting acid-free paper. When it is available, we choose paper that has been manufactured by environmentally responsible processes. These may include using trees grown in sustainable forests, incorporating recycled paper, minimizing chlorine in bleaching, or recycling the energy produced at the paper mill.

Library of Congress Cataloging-in-Publication Data
Bamburg, Jill, 1951–
    Getting to scale : growing your business without selling out / by Jill Bamburg.
      p. cm.
    Includes bibliographical references and index.
    ISBN-10: 1-57675-416-2; ISBN-13: 978-1-57675-416-0
    1. Small business—U.S.—Management—Case studies. 2. Entrepreneurship—U.S.—Case studies. 3. Social responsibility of business—U.S.—Case studies. 4. Success in business—U.S.— Case studies. I. Title.
HD62.7.B3537 2006
658.02'2—dc22   2006040792

First Edition
11 10 09 08 07 06   10 9 8 7 6 5 4 3 2 1

Interior Design: Gopa&Ted2, Inc.   Proofreader: Annette Jarvie
Copy Editor: Elissa Rabellino   Indexer: Medea Minnich
Production: Linda Jupiter, Jupiter Production

With gratitude to my parents,
Harold and Judy Bamburg

Contents

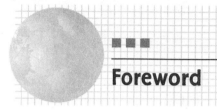

Foreword

JILL BAMBURG has taken a question critical to the future of our society and found compelling answers. She has brought them to life with rich, well-researched stories. The question is this: how can mission-driven companies grow to the size needed to make a significant difference without selling out their values? She finds nine critical issues that must be managed well to do so, and documents the secrets of success in managing each of them. This book will help anyone struggling with preserving his or her values as an enterprise grows.

Most books and courses on entrepreneurship focus on what it takes to start a business. They cover the forming of a team, writing a business plan, raising money, and so forth. These are important issues, but equally important issues arise once the venture is off the ground. This book lays out the principles for dealing with the critical issues that must be managed if a small mission-driven business is to grow to a significant size.

Jill comes to her knowledge of mission-driven business through personal experience as well as thorough research. We served together on the board of *In Context* magazine as it went through a flirtation with bankruptcy and a turbulent transition to rebirth as *Yes!* magazine. Together we learned the power of organic growth by supporting Fran Korten as she steadily grew *Yes!* to a financially stable size.

After *Yes!* became stable, Jill joined my wife and me in launching the Bainbridge Graduate Institute, one of the first business schools devoted to transforming business toward sustainability and social justice. From the beginning, Jill has led the development and delivery of our MBA in sustainable business. With few resources, she has created a 19-course program that has earned an impeccable national reputation and an average annual growth rate of 92 percent.

Having been with Jill through the growth of two mission-driven organizations, I was thrilled when she announced that she was writing a book on bringing mission-driven businesses to scale. This is a very important book. It is both a brilliant how-to book on what mission-driven businesses must do to grow with their values intact, and a description of what I hope is the future of large sections of our economy.

While a friend of the movement for local living economies, Jill is also a realist. Despite their large numbers, the small mission-driven organizations that abound today do not yet add up to a driving force in our economy. However, if a large number of them grow to a scale where they can compete effectively with the soulless giants, companies that keep their ethics and ideals intact can become the dominant force in our economic system. This book provides the tools that make that change possible.

Today our society, including hospitals, media, the government, and even universities, is increasingly structured around the needs of big business. One popular vision of the future is a world dominated by businesses whose leaders do nothing to promote healthy ecosystems, social justice, communities, or human health and happiness except as those issues impact their bottom line. Somehow the invisible hand of the free market is supposed to take all that greed and produce a healthy society.

I believe our world has become so complex that only self-organizing systems like free markets can create the order we need. Large-scale planned economies do not work. However, I also believe that free markets will function effectively only if the people in them behave as whole people, caring about the impact of their companies and their work on society, community, and planet.

Fortunately, values-driven organizations have a great advantage: they can recruit, motivate, and retain people who want to make a living and serve their values at the same time. But this advantage will drive the transformation of our economy only if we find ways to grow mission-driven businesses to scale.

Without that growth, which depends on the broad dissemination of the lessons contained in this book, our future could be coldhearted and unhealthy, filled with ravaged environments and destroyed communities, and made fearsome by the crime, terrorism, and war that come from a growing gap between rich and poor. Businesses whose missions include contributing to environmental health and social justice can help to build a warmhearted world, filled with healthy communities and healthy ecosystems. Jill Bamburg shows us the way to a brighter future, in which businesses care about their impact on the larger society.

After reading this book, entrepreneurs of mission-driven ventures will be able to grow their businesses, taking market share and profitability from businesses that are motivated by profit only. Students will learn that they can build a career that serves their values rather than compromising those values. People dreaming of building mission-driven enterprises will gain courage and insight from the stories of those who have successfully done it before.

Please get this book into the hands of anyone who has a mission-driven business. Give it to educators, students, and people who are losing their faith in free enterprise. Give it to anyone considering a career in business that serves more than his or her financial needs. You *can* succeed in business with your values in full expression, and reap the joy that comes from doing so, particularly after you reduce the risks by learning the secrets contained in this book. ▪ ▪

Gifford Pinchot III

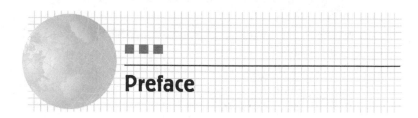

Preface

I BEGAN THINKING and dreaming about this book five years before I actually started working on it. At that time, I observed two trends that made a deep impression on me, and the relationship between them created the friction that eventually produced this book.

The first of these was the disturbing sale of a number of high-profile socially responsible businesses to larger companies that had no apparent commitment to anything other than the traditional financial bottom line. The second was the rise of a movement for local living economies, which seemed to cede whole huge sectors of the economy to traditional corporations in the interest of supporting smaller, community-based providers of selected goods and services.

I was left with two concerns: One was that the focus on local living economies would be fine as far as it went but would end up being too little, too late in terms of saving the planet from the ravages of the dominant big-business approach. The other was that there might be some fundamental flaw in the way we were approaching "socially responsible business"—something that forced firms to sell out once they became large enough to actually make a difference.

I mentioned these preoccupations to my friend David Korten, author of *When Corporations Rule the World* (2001), and he in turn mentioned them to his publisher, Steve Piersanti, of Berrett-Koehler, who eventually agreed to become my publisher as well.

I am deeply grateful to both of them for their unwavering belief in me and this book.

That was the beginning of my journey. Along the way, I met all manner of interesting people who were managing to pick their way to prosperity and scale without losing their souls or their commitment to service. It was tremendously inspiring to hear their stories; it is a powerful privilege to be able to share them. My hope is that they will offer just the right mix of inspiration and practicality to help the next batch of socially minded entrepreneurs get to scale—that is, grow to a size that is both economically viable and significant.

As I continued my journey and the book took shape, I found myself thinking more and more about the audience for these stories—not just today's mission-driven entrepreneurs but tomorrow's. In my day job, I am an educator. I manage and teach in the MBA program in sustainable business at the Bainbridge Graduate Institute (BGI), near Seattle, Washington. Our students are midcareer professionals, people going back to school to gain the skills and networks needed to align their work with their values— to find their vocation, if you will. I knew that they—and the millions of other midlife seekers hoping to reinvent their work lives in a spirit of service—would be inspired by these stories.

But even more than inspiring my own BGI students and my fellow there's-got-to-be-more-to-life-than-this boomers, I wanted to address the next generation of MBA students: the ones in the "mainstream" business schools where the best and the brightest are encouraged to check their values at the door and sign on to Milton Friedman's dictum that the "social responsibility of business is to increase its profits."[1]

Before writing this book, I was offended by that idea. After writing this book, I am outraged. How dare we tell the people who may ultimately determine the future of the planet that the highest purpose of their efforts is to maximize shareholder value!

While this remains the party line of many business school faculty members, it is grossly out of touch with the needs of the world. Fortunately, it is also out of touch with the desires and beliefs of a growing number of today's business school students. Particularly gratifying is the growing strength of Net Impact,

> . . . a network of more than 13,000 new-generation leaders committed to using the power of business to improve the world. It is also one of the most innovative and influential networks of MBAs, graduate students and young professionals in existence today. Our members believe that business can both earn a profit and create positive social change.[2]

It is my goal to carry the message of this book—that *another business world is possible*—to as many current and future practitioners of business as I possibly can. The people who are profiled in this book have found a way to conduct their businesses to serve people and planet, and to put profit in its proper place: as the fuel for further service. Let them be a lesson to all of us!

This is my first book, and one of its many lessons has been that it takes a village to write a book. I am fortunate to have such a village, some of whose members deserve particular mention.

First, I must thank my daughter, Katie Gao, for being the physical embodiment of my hope for the future—and for being such a darned good kid during the many months this book took me away from her.

Second, I thank my friends Dave and Fran Korten, and Gifford and Libba Pinchot, two couples who believed in me before I believed in myself and who have given me many wonderful opportunities to rise to their expectations.

Third, I thank the many people who provided direct aid in either the creation of this book or the management of my life during its creation: my co-parent, Ellen Connolly; research associate, Kate McDill; transcriptionist, M.A. Didrion; Berrett-Koehler reviewers, Chuck Ehrlich, Thomas Greco, and Jon Naar; copy editor extraordinaire, Elissa Rabellino; production manager, Linda Jupiter; pastoral cheerleader, Jeanne Pupke; and muse, Elizabeth von der Ahe.

Finally, I thank the entrepreneurs who shared their inspiring stories; my students, who continue to share their inspiring dreams; the staff at Berrett-Koehler, who are helping to make my own dreams come true; and you, my readers, for your own dreams and stories.

Together, we *can* change the way the world does business. But first we've got to get to scale. ■ ■

Jill Bamburg
Bainbridge Island, Washington, 2006

There IS Another Way

BEN & JERRY'S	STONYFIELD FARM	THE BODY SHOP
FOUNDED: 1978	FOUNDED: 1983	FOUNDED: 1976
SOLD: 2000	SOLD: 2001	SOLD: 2002/06

THREE SOCIALLY RESPONSIBLE BUSINESSES, three iconoclastic sets of entrepreneurs, three epic journeys, a single shared end: sale of the company to a new group of owners, an end to the era of founder control, and serious questions about the future of each company's commitment to the values that made it special. In the case of Ben & Jerry's, the founders were forced out by a decision of the public shareholders to sell to Unilever. With Stonyfield Farm, the owner decided to sell to one of its multinational competitors, Groupe Danone, in an effort to extend its reach. The Body Shop went public in 1984 but remained closely held and controlled by its founders until the early 2000s, when they tried, unsuccessfully, to sell the company and subsequently removed themselves from day-to-day operations. In March 2006, the firm was acquired by the French cosmetics giant, L'Oréal.

The three stories hit my personal radar in close enough proximity to make me wonder whether there was a fundamental flaw in our thinking about socially responsible business. Was there something peculiar to these businesses that made it impossible for them to stay independent and still grow to scale? Was the whole socially responsible business movement doomed to remain marginalized in the land of mom-and-pops? Would we have to give up our dream of changing the world by changing the way the world does business?

Or were there alternatives?

This book began with more questions than answers. The overriding question was whether (and how) socially responsible businesses could "scale up" without compromising their core values. Specifically:

- Could they compete on price while absorbing social and environmental costs?
- Could they obtain financing for their multiple-bottom-line values from single-bottom-line sources?
- Could they grow big enough to matter without losing the essential values of their "small is beautiful" corporate cultures?
- Could they be good global competitors without becoming bad local citizens?
- Could they build new cooperative structures that would successfully compete with conventional economies of scale?
- Could the businesses be sold without selling out their values?

These are some of the questions this book attempts to answer for entrepreneurs who are struggling with them in the present—or hoping to be successful enough to struggle with them in the future.

As Ben Cohen and Jerry Greenfield wrote in their business biography, *Ben & Jerry's Double-Dip,*

> [We] believed that business was a machine for making money. Therefore we thought the best way to make Ben & Jerry's a force for progressive social change was to grow bigger so we could make more profits and give more money away. We'd decided to give away 10 percent of our profits every year. Ten percent of the profits of a $100 million company could do a lot more good than 10 percent of the $3 [million] or $4 million we were currently doing. . . . We decided to go to the next level.[1]

For many mission-driven entrepreneurs, the desire to "go to the next level" in order to do more good in the world is equivalent to the conventional entrepreneur's desire to grow the business in order to make more money. Sometimes the desire to grow is based on a desire to give away more money, as it was for Ben and Jerry; more frequently, it's based on a desire to extend the benefits of the business's core environmental or social value proposition to a broader market. And in some cases, for mission-driven entrepreneurs as well as their more financially driven counterparts, growth is an imperative—not a choice. In some industries, "grow or die" is a fundamental business reality, whether they like it or not.

Gary Hirschberg, the legendary CEO of Stonyfield Farm, the organic yogurt company that he sold in 2001 to multinational Groupe Danone, ran into those dynamics long before the company sold:

> Our problem was that the yogurt was a huge hit. The demand far exceeded what we could produce. But we were losing money on every sale. . . . Commercial yogurt making is very capital intensive. This was not about getting big. It was about getting to a scale that could be profitable.
>
> Also, you face the problem that supermarkets charge slotting fees to carry your product. . . . Once you enter the supermarket—but by no means do I want to implicate only the supermarket—once you're in the marketplace, unfortunately, the pie theory takes over. The universe is only so big; the market is only so big. And if you don't grow, and someone is growing faster than the market, then you shrink. In other words, your slice shrinks. And unfortunately, shelf space—which is the Holy Grail in my business—and shelf position, which is a subset of shelf space—are completely dependent on who's delivering more profitability.
>
> You know, the supermarket's little secret of my business is that they don't make money selling food, they make it selling real estate. And you have to be competitive to even hold your place, let alone grow it.[2]

I began this book with three theoretical perspectives on scale. The first had to do with conventional economies of scale and whether those realities might somehow be at odds with the ideals of social enterprise or mission-driven firms. The second pertained to the "small is beautiful" arguments originally made by E. F. Schumaker in the 1970s[3] and recently extended by Michael Shuman and others to embrace the idea that "local is beautiful."[4] The concern there was whether the intrinsic values of "small" and "local" might somehow trump the virtues of scale—that big might be bad, period. The third was a set of ideas, coming from multiple sources, that had to do with "mass customization"[5] and notions about "appropriate" scale. Were there, perhaps, some intermediate approaches that could combine the virtues of both big and small?

Conventional Economies of Scale

While it is popular among some business critics to argue that the drive for growth is fueled by simple greed and power lust, that argument has at best only partial validity. Much of the drive toward growth in business has to do with economies of scale, a value-neutral idea that is both simple and intuitive: in many (but not all) production systems, the more units you produce, the less each unit costs.

The classic example of economies of scale is the proverbial widget factory with a set of fixed costs that remain the same regardless of the number of widgets produced. It costs a certain amount of money to build the plant, turn on the lights, run the equipment, warehouse the inventory, ship goods to market, and sell the goods to customers. While some of these costs are variable—that is, directly related to the volume of goods produced— many others are not. They are the same whether the factory produces a hundred widgets or a thousand.

What changes with volume is the amount of these fixed costs, or overhead, that must be covered by each unit sold. If the fixed costs are, say, $100,000, and the plant produces 100 units, each unit must be priced to recover $1,000 in fixed costs alone. But if the same plant produces 1,000 units, each unit can be priced to recover only $100 in fixed costs. In competitive, capital-intensive industries, such economies of scale frequently determine the winners and losers.

But the concept of scale is by no means limited to manufacturing operations. Economies of scale, including those sometimes referred to as economies of "scope,"[6] are a factor in most, if not all, businesses. It costs a certain amount of money to open a store, hire an employee, buy a truck, build a computer system, or install a phone line—and those costs are the same whether the store is crowded or empty, the employee is busy or idle, the truck is empty or full, the computer system is processing 100 transactions or 1,000, the phone is handling 3 calls or 300.

But the advantages of scale extend well beyond the ability to recover fixed costs. Bigger enterprises have a much easier time commanding the attention of suppliers, channel partners, and customers. On the supply side, companies that get to scale are able to earn volume discounts and favorable terms. In the channel, those companies can afford to pay the slotting fees and build the consumer demand that secures a bigger and better position on the shelf. And on the consumer side, size confers an advantage in the ability to reduce prices (thereby further increasing volume) and spend more money on marketing.

All this matters to the mission-driven entrepreneur because some of our most deeply held mission commitments—to local employment and livable wages, company cultures that feel more communal than corporate, organic products grown close to home—fly in the face of conventional economies of scale. The challenge is to find a way to maintain those commitments while meeting or beating the competition and, at the same time, to "scale up" our enterprises to serve larger groups of customers and have a greater impact on the economy as a whole.

Fortunately, the difficulty of this challenge is partially ameliorated by the diseconomies of scale that are also inherent in larger enterprises. These diseconomies are sometimes purely

a creation of management in the form of bureaucratic deci-
sion-making processes or excessive corporate overhead. A classic example is the situation of a product manager in a large
multiproduct, multinational enterprise who has difficulty getting the necessary corporate approvals to respond in a timely
manner to a local competitive threat. Many a wonderful
opportunity has been spawned in a niche that was too small or
unprofitable to be served by the 800-pound gorilla in a given
product category.[7]

In other cases, the diseconomies are a function of the very
capital investments that were supposed to lead to scale
economies. Even in an industry as scale driven as steel, technology advances have brought down the giants of history and
awarded the future to the upstart owners of the newer mini-mills.
When technology shifts, the traditional assets that created
economies of scale can quickly turn into huge liabilities. And
when markets shift rapidly—as increasingly they do—flexibility
may be far more important than scale in maintaining both customer satisfaction and overall profitability. This is good news for
small producers.

Potentially dwarfing all of these traditional diseconomies is
the emerging issue of transportation costs. Just as cheap transportation made globalization possible, so expensive transportation is likely to make localization more attractive. At some point,
the expected increase in transportation costs may very well over-
take the production savings in lower labor costs or capital-intensive global manufacturing facilities, leaving some of today's
large-scale competitors with "stranded assets"[8]—and creating
new opportunities for smaller local producers.

Although this is a book about scale and the drive to become
bigger, economic shifts that help smaller producers also help
values-based firms, largely because they reduce the need for outside capital, one of the most problematic issues for mission-
driven firms. Since most capital providers are still operating in a
single-bottom-line world, it is difficult to find investors who can
fully support the values and timetables of many mission-driven

firms. Anything that can be done to reduce a firm's dependence on outside capital is likely to increase its ability to hang on to its core values as it grows.

Small Is Beautiful

Going to scale is not for everyone. Beginning with E. F. Schumaker's highly influential 1973 book *Small Is Beautiful,* several generations of entrepreneurs have formally repudiated the drive for quantitative growth and made a compelling case for the personal, social, and (to a lesser extent) business benefits of remaining small. Today, such businesses are sometimes referred to as "lifestyle" businesses—that is, businesses that are driven by the owner's desire to live a certain kind of life or build a business reflecting a certain set of values—rather than by traditional financial imperatives. In many cases, "small" has also come to mean "local," and the lifestyle and values being championed are grounded in community.

One of the things that were most striking to me in my research was the extent to which the people I interviewed did *not* embody the small-is-beautiful ethos. By and large, they expressed remarkably little nostalgia for the Good Old Days of their small beginnings and very little ambivalence about the growth they had achieved. Because they had built their businesses to support values they believed in, they embraced growth. As long as they were able to maintain their focus on mission (which all of them were), bigger was better.

As Ray Codey, director of development at New Community Corporation, in Newark, New Jersey, put it, "Small is not necessarily beautiful if the problems are big."[9]

Appropriate Scale

The notion of appropriate scale is appealing. Bigger is not always better, and small is not always beautiful. Arguably, what matters is "right sizing"—being "big enough."

The answer for each organization lies somewhere at the intersection of mission and margin. The organization must be big enough to achieve its mission while maintaining a satisfactory financial return, whatever that may mean in any given instance. In thinking about this, it makes sense to keep in mind strategy guru Michael Porter's admonition to avoid getting "stuck in the middle."[10]

Many industries exhibit a U-shaped relationship between profitability and scale, as shown in the figure below.

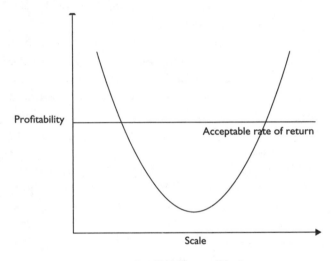

Profitability and Scale

As the figure shows, smaller niche players can be highly profitable, usually by charging a premium price; and larger, mass-market players can be highly profitable, usually through economies of scale. What is problematic is trying to achieve profitability between the two poles. As Michael Porter has written,

> The firm stuck in the middle is almost guaranteed low profitability. It either loses the high-volume customers who demand low prices or must bid away its profits to get this business away from low-cost firms. Yet it also loses the high-margin businesses—the cream—to the firms who are

focused on high-margin targets or have achieved differentiation overall. The firm stuck in the middle also probably
suffers from a blurred corporate culture and a conflicting
set of organizational arrangements and motivation system.[11]

An "appropriate scale" may thus be large or small, but will
probably not fall in between. This is an important point to keep
in mind when fashioning a strategy for going to scale—and it
may explain why so many promising small companies, mission-
driven or not, fail to make the transition.

About This Book

This book has two target audiences: today's successful mission-
driven entrepreneurs—and tomorrow's. I say "successful"
because I assume that an enterprise must have achieved some
level of success to have earned the right to grapple with questions of scale. As for tomorrow's mission-driven entrepreneurs,
I believe their chances of success will be greatly improved by
thinking ahead of time about issues of growth, scale, exit, and
legacy.

The book is organized around nine key lessons I took away
from two years of research and some 30 interviews with mission-
driven entrepreneurs who are succeeding in growing their businesses to scale. They are an inspiring bunch, and whenever
possible, I've let them use their own words to tell their stories.
The people and companies are listed at the end of this chapter.
A short summary of the nine lessons follows.

Mission comes first

It is no accident that the businesses included in this book are
called "mission *driven*." They truly are. Just as a relentless focus
on the bottom line helps to align and rationalize the decisions
in a financially driven firm, so the focus on mission serves as an
organizational plumb line in these firms.

▧ ▧ Any business can do it

This was the greatest surprise to me in the research for this book. I set out to cast a wide net in terms of industries and had absolutely no trouble finding mission-driven businesses in every segment I researched. Similarly, I thought that only some types of businesses would scale, but I found enough different approaches to growth to make me wonder whether that was true. Undoubtedly there are limits to both observations, but I didn't find them—and was heartened by that!

▧ ▧ Organic is the way to grow

This slower, more natural approach to growth came up over and over again, and my interviewees contrasted it with both the get-big-fast growth of the dot-com era and the target-driven growth models of conventionally trained MBAs. Mission-driven businesses tend to grow more slowly, and *need* to grow more slowly.

▧ ▧ Finance your independence

"Bootstrapping"—that is, financing business growth largely out of revenues—is a time-honored tradition among entrepreneurs (or was until the dot-com era planted a get-rich-quick alternative in the brains of an impressionable new generation). For mission-driven entrepreneurs, the critical issue is independence—not growth—and bootstrapping is the best way to preserve independence. Fortunately, it is not the *only* way.

▧ ▧ Build your values into the brand

It is a truism among green marketers that customers will *not* pay a premium for green products. On the other hand, all other things being equal (like the cardinal virtues of price, quality, and convenience), customers *will* choose values-based products over their competitors. And while customers won't pay a premium for green products, they *will* pay a premium for products perceived to be of higher quality along other dimensions. And that premium price frequently translates into bigger margins, which can be used to further the mission.

▪▪Match manufacturing to mission

The good news is this: it *is* possible to manufacture products in the United States at a competitive and affordable price! And it's also possible to manufacture products globally at prices even the poorest people can afford. Vertical integration, or owning multiple links in the value chain, appears to be the key. On the other hand, for mission-driven *brand* builders, outsourcing is the preferred manufacturing strategy—and makes it a whole lot easier to get started.

▪▪Morph early and often

As one of my mentors, intrapreneuring expert Gifford Pinchot III, likes to say, "There are no facts about the future." Therefore, a business plan, while theoretically a blueprint of the business, is essentially a form of fiction. Reality is almost always different. Successful social entrepreneurs hold the mission constant but allow the market to determine the course of the business.

▪▪Form follows function

Mission-driven ventures come in all different flavors: for-profit, nonprofit, hybrid, public, private, co-op, employee stock ownership plans (ESOPs), community development corporations (CDCs), and forms that have yet to be invented. Each has advantages and disadvantages, but any legal form can support a mission focus (even publicly traded corporations, although that's harder!).

▓ ▓ The soft stuff is the hardest

Most business schools make a distinction between the "hard" stuff—that is, the kinds of problems that lend themselves to quantitative analysis—and the "soft" stuff, the kinds of "touchy-feely" issues that come up anytime you work with people. And as every business practitioner knows, the most difficult problems are almost always the people problems. In mission-driven firms, culture is part of the answer—and part of the problem.

But all of that is the map, not the territory. And it's a rather crude map, abstracted from experience after the fact. What brings the territory alive are stories of the entrepreneurs who have actually made the journey and who may inspire the rest of us to strike out on our own.

Companies and Interviews

During the first half of 2005, I interviewed approximately 30 entrepreneurs who had succeeded in bringing their companies to scale. I identified them through magazine articles, Web research, membership in the Social Venture Network (SVN)[12] and Co-op America Business Network (CABN),[13] and personal connections. Whenever possible, I interviewed the founder or cofounder of the company, because I wanted to hear the whole story from the beginning to the present—how the company started, where it got its capital, what was easy, what was hard. I tried to ferret out new stories, ones that haven't been overtold, because I wanted to get beyond the usual suspects and make sure there was a broader base of practitioners.

There is, indeed, a broader base of practitioners—in both numbers and variety. They are an interesting and inspiring group, remarkably humble considering their accomplishments, and genuinely eager to share their lessons with others seeking to use business as a vehicle for effecting social change.

Interviews
Apparel
American Apparel Inc., Marty Bailey—VP, operations
Birkenstock USA, Margot Fraser—founder; retired CEO
Eileen Fisher Inc., Susan Schor—chief culture officer
Hemptown Clothing, Jason Finnis—founder; president

Computers and Electronics
GreenDisk, David Beschen—founder; CEO

Consumer Products
Gardener's Supply Company, Will Raap—founder; CEO
Give Something Back Business Products,[14] Mike Hannigan—
  cofounder; CEO
Green Glass Inc., Sean Penrith—cofounder; CEO
Organic Specialties Inc. (Citrisolve), Steve Zeitler—cofounder; CEO
Seventh Generation Inc., Jeffrey Hollender—founder; CEO
Tweezerman International, Dal LaMagna—founder
Wild Planet Toys Inc., Jennifer Chapman—COO

Economic Development
Endeavor, Blair Pillsbury—VP, Latin America; Louise Hulme—director,
  finance and administration
The Green Institute, Michael Krause—executive director
KickStart, Martin Fisher—cofounder
New Community Corporation, Msgr. William Linder—founder; CEO
Upstream 21, Leslie Christian—cofounder

Food
Cascadian Farm (General Mills),[15] Gene Kahn—founder;
  VP, sustainability
Country Natural Beef, Doc and Connie Hatfield—cofounders
Equal Exchange Inc., Rink Dickinson—cofounder; co-CEO
Frontier Natural Products Co-op, Andy Pauley—board chair; CEO
Great Harvest Bread Company,[16] Mike Ferretti—president; CEO
New Belgium Brewing Company, Kim Jordan—cofounder; CEO

Organic Valley Family of Farms, George Siemon—founder; CEO
Pura Vida Coffee, John Sage—cofounder; president
Small Potatoes Urban Delivery Inc. (SPUD), David Van Seters—
    founder; CEO
Stonyfield Farm,[17] Gary Hirshberg—founder

Medical
Project Impact Inc., David Green—founder
ScriptSave, Charlie Horn—founder; chairman

Paper
New Leaf Paper, Jeff Mendelsohn—founder; CEO

Services
Bright Horizons Family Solutions Inc., Linda Mason—cofounder;
    chairman
Trillium Asset Management Corporation, Joan Bavaria—founder; CEO
Village Real Estate Services, Mark Deutschmann—founder; owner
Working Assets, Laura Scher—cofounder; CEO

Transportation
Flexcar, Lance Ayrault—president; CEO
Novex Couriers, Rob Safrata—president; CEO
Westport Innovations Inc., David Demers—CEO

CHAPTER ONE

Mission
Comes First

WORKING ASSETS, best known as a telecommunications company supporting progressive nonprofits, was 20 years old and generating $100 million in annual revenues when I popped the killer question to CEO and cofounder Laura Scher.

"So what about values conflicts?" I wanted to know. Were there times when she wanted to do business with people who shared her values but found that she couldn't because another company was a better fit from a business perspective? Were there conflicts between the need to grow and the desire to maintain the feeling of a smaller firm? Conflicts between competing values? Had there been issues like that during her history with Working Assets?

Amazingly enough, her answer was no.

> Nothing comes to mind where we've had tradeoffs like that. . . . Maybe it's that we never even entertained it. . . . I think it's possible that we don't even look at things that wouldn't be true to our mission.[1]

Sean Penrith, a South African entrepreneur now living in the United States, had a similar answer. The cofounder of Green Glass, a successful international firm that turns recycled bottles into elegant glassware, said,

> I think there are occasions where one can do certain things to accelerate either growth or revenue which are not purely

. . . it's not that they're not ethical, it's just that they're not ethical to us. So we don't do that.

For the most part, we all agree, but there are a couple of us that say, "Well, hey, we're here to drive a business and this is called marketing." I'd rather stick with what I think is correct.[2]

A similar answer came from George Siemon, founder and CEO of Organic Valley Family of Farms, an agricultural co-op with 18 years in business and $245 million in sales. On the values-conflict question:

They're not necessarily conflicts; they're just decisions we've had to make. Maybe we'd have been better for this or that, but they've been guiding principles that we have that have defined our business.[3]

It is no accident that these businesses—and the others included in this book—are called "mission *driven*." They truly are. Just as a relentless focus on the bottom line helps to align and rationalize the decisions in a financially driven firm, so the focus on mission serves as an organizational plumb line in these firms. Here, profit is not the purpose of business—or even a byproduct or measure of success. Rather, it is a means to an end: the furtherance of mission—support for family farms, progressive nonprofits, community development, the elimination of poverty, or other good causes.

When the company's consumer value proposition is directly tied to the firm's social value proposition, it becomes a lot easier to make day-to-day business decisions, to avoid values conflicts, and to address the "legacy" issues to ensure that the social values of the firm will outlive the founder's direct involvement. The pieces fit together and reinforce each other in a way that is almost magical.

Small Potatoes Urban Delivery Inc. (SPUD)

David Van Seters's Small Potatoes Urban Delivery Inc. (SPUD), a home delivery business for organic food in Vancouver, British Columbia, is a case in point. Van Seters, an environmentalist with an MBA, started SPUD after making a systematic search for a business idea that could be implemented on a relatively small scale and would allow him to integrate his environmental and social values with his business practices. Through a consulting contract, he said,

> I became much more aware of the rapid decline of the family farm and small-scale food processors, how little money farmers actually get of the retail food dollar. After they've worked at growing the crop and nurturing it and have that finished product in their hands, they only get 10 to 20 cents on the dollar for it. I also realized how much power in the food industry is controlled at the retail level, and that alternative distribution channels have the potential to create a better return for the farmer while not increasing costs for the consumer.
>
> At that point I thought, wow, this business really would integrate environmental, economic, and social values, because we could deliver groceries at no extra cost to the consumer and at the same time protect the environment by delivering organic and locally sourced natural foods and enabling customers to avoid the pollution and traffic congestion of driving to their local store. And in terms of social values, we're helping boost the local economy and helping to support small local family farms and small-scale food processors that were rapidly going out of business.[4]

■ ■

SMALL POTATOES URBAN DELIVERY INC.

Years in Business:	8 (founded in 1998)
Start-up Capital:	$200,000
Annual Sales (2005):	$10 million (Canadian)
Corporate Form:	Private for-profit
Business:	Organic home delivery service

■ ■

Webvan and HomeGrocer.com, the two big online grocery-delivery services, together burned through $1 billion in cash before going into bankruptcy. Where they focused on money, Van Seters focused on mission. In the end, he thinks that focus was a large part of why he succeeded and they did not.

I think the biggest reason we succeeded is that we didn't come from a grocery background. We relied instead on our general business knowledge and a sustainability focus.

Our competitors were trying to duplicate the in-store shopping experience, which is that the customer can shop almost whenever they want, and can get almost any product that they want. It turns out that the costs of doing that are too high and the customer is not willing to pay those costs. Delivering to people whenever they want within a two-hour window is very inefficient from a fossil-fuel perspective because the drivers might have to go all across town to deliver to one customer, and then have to come all the way back to deliver to the next customer and then have to return to the location of the first customer to complete the third delivery.

So what we've said is we deliver to each neighborhood only once per week, and the customer doesn't have to be home for their delivery. As a result, instead of spending $9 to do an average delivery, which is what it costs the Internet grocery companies, we can do it for less than $3. And in fact, the savings are so great that we don't actually charge a delivery fee so long as the customer orders at least $35 worth of groceries. The big Internet grocery companies told their customers, "Your groceries will cost you exactly the same as shopping in-store, but you have to pay a $7 to $10 delivery fee on each delivery." It turns out that very few customers are willing to pay this delivery fee.

The other thing they did was offer a huge range of products, which made the logistics of receiving and shipping and packing untenable, because they couldn't pack an average order in less than 24 minutes. It just took too much time. You just don't have enough efficiencies in the system to accommodate taking 24 minutes to pack an average order. In contrast, by offering a good but narrower product selection, we can pack an order in under 7 minutes.

The third biggest reason for our success is our social mission. For example, our customers could see how we were benefiting the farmer because we would write articles about them: how they were started and why they chose to produce certain crops. Our customers really responded to that. They believed that they were getting different products with a different ethic behind them.

Even in the early years when our Web site didn't work that well and we made mistakes on packing because we really didn't know what we were doing, they stuck with us. As one customer described the SPUD difference, "It's like getting free karma with every delivery."

So while the big Internet companies enjoyed initial excitement from consumers, those customers dropped off really quickly because as soon as the delivery didn't fit their needs perfectly, they didn't have any loyalty. With us, they actually made a commitment and stayed with us and grew with us so that we actually survived when most of the big players failed.[5]

In the case of SPUD, even the difficult challenge of finding appropriate financing—one of the major issues for all mission-driven firms—worked in favor of the company's focus on values. SPUD was founded with an initial investment from Renewal Partners Venture Fund, which focuses on businesses with a social or environmental mission. Since then, it has taken on an additional 22 socially minded individual investors. Traditional investors and lenders wouldn't touch the deal because it wasn't exciting enough during the dot-com boom and was considered too risky after the dot-com bust.

As a result, the company was significantly undercapitalized, which also contributed to its success—particularly in contrast to its dot-com counterparts. Van Seters observed,

> Their whole model was to get to volume first and then get to profitability. That was a very risky approach. And, in fact, everyone looking back at the dot-com era can't believe how so many investors were duped with a strategy that never worked in history. You always get to profitability first and then grow.

> One of the founders of HomeGrocer said that their preference would have been to get to profitability first, but they had generated all this money through their IPO and the investors were clamoring for rapid returns, so they had to grow quickly and were forced to expand to multiple cities before they got to profitability. Of course, when the dot-com era crashed and there was no more investment money around, none of the locations were near profitability. So they ran out of cash within six months and had no choice but to close their doors.

> In contrast, we had always said, "Let's get to profitability first and then grow from that point." So we only raised a small amount of money, and therefore had to use every bit of it as best we could. We got to profitability in about three years, and we've been profitable ever since.[6]

So far, so good. But now Van Seters is beginning to tackle the next challenge of scale. The single biggest capital investment behind SPUD is the sophisticated computer system that makes the whole business work. The initial investments in the system cost roughly $1.5 million, and Van Seters estimates that he spends another $250,000 per year in maintenance and improvements—the costs of which must be amortized over a business that operates on a 1 percent margin. Already, SPUD has acquired 12 of its smaller competitors—all at their request, largely because they simply couldn't afford the information technology (IT) investments required to offer a competitive service.

Van Seters has set his sights on expansion into the U.S. market, beginning with Seattle. The arguments for going to scale come from the perspective of both money and mission. On the one hand, there's a need to amortize the fixed costs of the IT investments; on the other, there's a desire to expand a workable model of community-based organic agriculture to other markets. But implicit in the latter is an inherent conflict with another important value: local ownership.

This is an issue near and dear to Van Seters's heart, and one to which he's given a lot of thought. He believes that what he is exporting is a business model that may eventually work as a locally owned franchise and that in the meantime extracts only 1 percent of its revenues from the local community.

> Generally, to make a franchise work, you have to have a pretty cookie-cutter business, something where you can give someone a manual that provides details about the size of the warehouse, the size of the coolers, the number of racks, the computer system, the packing procedures, and so on.
>
> We're still in a rapid learning phase, where we haven't got the model finalized enough. We're still customizing our information systems and our procedures on a weekly basis. Once that settles down, if it settles down, and we actually say, "OK, we've got a model that would work under different settings, different demographics, different locations," then we would be more confident about franchising. Certainly, we're not against franchising.

Because we only make about a 1 percent profit, 99 percent of that money stays in that local market. In addition, we offer profit sharing and weekly bonuses in all our markets. Further, some staff have become equity shareholders in the company. So, even the meager profits that we get, those are distributed back out to the local offices.

In terms of the overarching philosophy of buying local and supporting small companies, we have the view that we are primarily transporting a business model to different locations. We are hiring locally, we're buying locally, and we're sourcing our products locally. Our goal is to try to buy at least 50 percent of our product from the local area, wherever that is.[7]

▪▪ LESSONS LEARNED

The SPUD story is one of my favorites because it embodies so many practical lessons in a single inspiring tale. SPUD directly aligns the interests of producers and consumers, and does good things for the planet while serving both. It manages a complex home delivery system in a way that conserves fossil fuels while saving customers money. It offers a more narrowly defined service than its dot-com predecessors but produces greater customer satisfaction.

There is a kind of magic at work in the SPUD story and in many of the stories included in this book. It is a magic that happens when mission is placed at the center of the business, and the triple-bottom-line objectives of people, planet, and profit become mutually reinforcing. In more traditional business thinking, people and planet are seen as nice-to-haves, but profit comes first. There is a tension among the three objectives, and the challenge of managing to a triple bottom line of people, planet, and profit is the challenge of managing the trade-offs among them.

Not so with SPUD and other mission-driven firms that have found—or, more precisely, created—a sweet spot in the market where the values of the triple bottom line intersect and reinforce each other.[8] The mission of SPUD is "to be the most socially responsible, environmentally sound, *and* financially profitable internet home delivery company in North America *while* simplifying and enriching the lives of our customers, staff, suppliers, and community partners [emphases mine]."[9] There are no trade-offs here: the people of SPUD want to have it all. And it is this commitment to a complex and multifaceted mission that is the source of the organization's creativity and success. ■ ■

CHAPTER TWO

Any Business
Can Do It

EVERY INDUSTRY IS DIFFERENT. Customers and competitors, products and production systems, supply chains and distribution networks, and a host of other variables all differ from one industry to the next.

When I started this book, one of my questions was whether a mission-driven approach could work in any industry—or would be successful only in a handful of industries with very particular characteristics. At the conclusion of my research, I can't say for certain that a values-based approach will work in *every* industry, but I can say that there are values-based companies in every segment I investigated. And as you can see from the list in the introduction, I investigated a broad range of industries.

The follow-up question was a little trickier: what makes it easy or hard to stay mission driven in any given segment? To address that question, I took a closer look at companies in five different industries, selected to create as varied a sampling as possible. Then I arranged them along a continuum based on a purely informal and subjective assessment of the difficulty each experienced in maintaining its values focus.

The array I came up with is on the following page.

As I played with this further, I was able to deduce two broad criteria that had led to these placements:

- The extent to which the external marketplace supported the firms' differentiation based on mission.
- The extent to which the internal business logic of the firm reinforced the values of the founder.

25

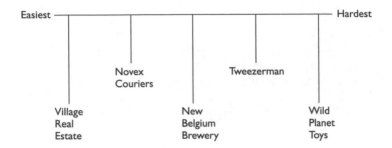

Difficulty of Maintaining Mission Focus

The important corollary to this analysis has to do with the so-called legacy problem,[1] a term originated (or at least popularized) by *Business Ethics* editor Marjorie Kelly and used to describe the difficulties of maintaining the values of a mission-driven company after the founder's departure. The first criterion suggests a bit of advice that will be repeated over and over again in this book: build the values of the mission directly into the brand. This was an important part of the strategy of Village Real Estate Services and Novex Couriers, the two companies at the "easier" end of the spectrum. The second criterion suggests a different piece of advice: build execution of the mission into the core operation and cost structure of the business so that it is not simply a nice-to-have that can be lopped off to save money when times get tough.

But just because something is "easier" or "easiest" on a relative scale doesn't mean it's easy in any absolute way. With that caveat in mind, it will be useful to consider these ventures as they appear along the continuum.

Village Real Estate Services

The real estate industry is about the last place I would have looked for a mission-driven business—period. And to think that this industry would be the source of the firm with the greatest internal and external support for mission was a real surprise. Nonetheless, in Nashville, Tennessee, Mark Deutschmann has built a brilliant mission-driven business in his for-profit Village Real Estate Services and nonprofit Village Fund.

. . . .

VILLAGE REAL ESTATE SERVICES

Years in business:	10 (founded in 1996)
Start-up capital:	$250,000
Annual sales (2005):	$340 million
Corporate form:	Hybrid: Village Real Estate Services is private for-profit; the Village Fund is a nonprofit
Business:	Residential real estate

. . . .

A real estate broker by trade, Deutschmann became a social entrepreneur by association—in his case, association with the Social Venture Network (SVN), a shared affiliation of the four U.S. entrepreneurs in this chapter and many of the others featured throughout the book.[2] In 1996, Deutschmann was about to open a new office for the real estate firm he worked with at the time, when he attended a workshop that gave him some time for writing and reflection.

> Basically, I wanted to take some of the values I was seeing interpreted through businesses by SVN members [and] bring some of that to the real estate industry. I had been searching my soul, wondering what kind of business I could start that had social values and a socially responsible mission, but also I was becoming fairly successful in the practice of real estate here in Nashville, Tennessee, and thought, why shouldn't I just try to bring some value into an industry that's already well established and try to shift the real estate industry? That's where Village got started.[3]

There are two critical ways in which Village expresses the values of its founder. The first is in its market focus. While most real estate firms seek business wherever they can find it and thus end up selling a lot of new housing units that contribute to urban sprawl, Deutschmann focused Village on "the real estate consumer seeking alternatives to cookie-cutter houses and urban sprawl. . . . With its attention to community, Village strives to attract customers and agents who prefer living and working in neighborhoods where people interact and care for each other."[4] The firm has built a specialty in "recycling" houses in older, established neighborhoods and in selling—and, more recently, developing—urban in-fill and condo/loft units downtown.

The second way in which Village is unique is in its establishment of the nonprofit Village Fund, an organization that "supports nonprofit initiatives that contribute to positive sustainable growth, citizen empowerment and social change."[5] The fund owns a percentage of the for-profit venture, receives dividends along with the other owners, and also receives a donation from every real estate transaction.

One of the most interesting wrinkles in the story of the fund is the way in which it is scaling up as the for-profit grows and expands its influence in the real estate community. In addition to the contributions that Village Real Estate Services makes to the fund, many of its sales agents—now a hundred strong—also make donations from their individual commissions on each transaction they make. Village encourages its buyers and sellers to make similar donations, and, most important, it has established a program called Community Builder that encourages the vendors with which it does business—banks, attorneys, mortgage companies, title companies, escrow companies, and other entities involved in real estate transactions—to make a donation for the fees they receive on every Village deal.

The fund is completely aligned with the market positioning of the real estate company and actually strengthens its brand while doing good work. According to Deutschmann,

> I think there's a place where we continue to show that we have a unique selling proposition in the community, and

the Village Fund is one of those pieces. We're quite involved in a lot of the downtown and midtown initiatives, and talking about the things that the Civic Design Center and the Nashville Downtown Partnership are promoting for our good urban core—becoming a bike-friendly, walkable city. I think the stuff we're doing is actually increasing our market share. We're creating value in the kinds of things that we'd like to promote. So even if we're absorbed or merged or something like that, [the acquirer] wouldn't want to dry up the values because it's one of the things that caused us to be successful.[6]

Novex Couriers

In Vancouver, British Columbia, Rob Safrata is living his values through Novex Couriers, his third entrepreneurial venture. There was nothing particularly environmentally or socially responsible about Nova Messenger Services when Safrata and his business partners bought it out of receivership in 2000. They spent the first six months getting it back to breakeven, and the next year and a half running it as a conventional courier service making same-day deliveries around the Vancouver area. Once the day-to-day operations were under control, Safrata went out into the marketplace to figure out what was next.

My role in our group is as the entrepreneur. I [asked] a number of leaders what was important in Vancouver, and they all said sustainability.

So my job is to be curious and to connect the dots and look for ways to build the business and lead the business. I realized that we could do something about this because we had a hundred vehicles—and not very nice vehicles. They pollute a lot! And there were a number of other [environmental improvement opportunities] throughout the company—the paper and the water and electricity and the carpet and the coffee and on and on.

I started doing research, presented the research to our company . . . and as we got more information, it became very compelling. It was painfully obvious where we weren't behaving very well and where we could make a difference. And once we had that information, we went from "can do something" to "should do something"—and pretty soon [we] realized that we must become evangelists and try to do everything that we can. And while some people say, "You're doing a great job," we realized that we're not even close to what we need to be doing and what most people should be doing, or will have to do soon.[7]

Specifically, Safrata did an environmental audit that made some of the next steps obvious, such as the acquisition of a set of hybrid and natural gas-powered vehicles, which now make up 20 percent of the Novex fleet. The company estimates that its 17 hybrids alone save nearly 1,000 pounds of CO_2 emissions *per day*.[8] These vehicles, part of the Novex Clean initiative, serve as mobile billboards reminding local residents of Novex's ongoing source of differentiation. Those mobile billboards, plus the tremendous press that Novex has gotten for being "the first and only courier committed to reducing the environmental impact of our operations," have paid off handsomely in the marketplace for both customers and employees.

NOVEX COURIERS

Years in business:	28 (founded in 1978); 6 years under current owners (bought in 2000)
Start-up capital:	NA
Annual sales (2005):	$6.5 million (Canadian)
Corporate form:	Private for-profit
Business:	Courier service

For smaller customers with compatible values, the switch to Novex has been a no-brainer. For larger companies, in which the sales cycle is longer and more complex, the selection of Novex has sometimes been spearheaded by a CEO who wanted to make his or her own environmental statement. And when there's a problem, the Novex Clean program is a tremendous source of customer loyalty, said Safrata.

> We have about 2,500 opportunities to make a mistake every day. And we've had a number of customers who at some point would have switched. That happens all the time—one bad day and they say, "We're switching." [But now] they say, "Well, that was unfortunate. Let's talk about how we can make sure it doesn't happen again. And we're using you because it's more important than this one mistake."
>
> The pride in our company has tripled. The fact that we are doing something every day, people say, "Yeah, we're making a difference. I'm with a good company." And when we are hiring people, we are able to attract people who never would even look at our company before or our industry—in the finance department, in the sales department, and in operations—because of the way we're doing things. So that was huge.[9]

For all those benefits, however, Novex has not positioned itself as a premium courier at a premium price. The business is very competitive, said Safrata.

> Price is always an issue, so we don't charge more for this. We don't go up at the front and say, "Hey, we're environmental." We go through the business points first: service, technology, and price. And then we say, "And, by the way, here's an important benefit. Is this important to you?"[10]

The final thing worth noting about the Novex experience is that it really hasn't cost the company much money to "do the right thing." This is where the business logic supports the mission.

> [Figuring out what to do] cost a fair amount of money. But once we made the shift, that's just the way we do business now. And it's a great way to do business. Nothing we did cost more money to do. In some cases, it cost less. Or with equipment—we were able to make an equivalent [amount] or have a quick payback of what it actually cost.[11]

Both Village Real Estate Services and Novex Couriers fall at the "easier" end of the spectrum because their mission is directly built into their brand, or value proposition to consumers. Each has also built its mission directly into the business logic of its operations: in the network of business partnerships created around the Village Fund, in the case of Village Real Estate Services, and in the hybrid vehicles that make up the fleet—and provide the advertising—for Novex Couriers. If either business were to change hands, the branded and embedded mission would be an important asset in the transaction, thereby helping to ensure its continuation.

New Belgium Brewing Company

The story of New Belgium is an entrepreneurial classic. Young American man goes bicycling in Europe, falls in love with Belgian beer. Begins home brewing in his basement, falls in love with young woman, decides to take beer operation commercial. The couple takes a second mortgage on their house, max out a batch of credit cards, outgrow their basement operation—and just keep on growing. In 1992, their first full year of production, Jeff Lebesch and Kim Jordan brewed just under a thousand barrels. In 2005, they brewed 370,300 barrels, making New Belgium the third-largest craft brewery in the United States and the 11th-largest brewery in the United States.[12]

■ ■

NEW BELGIUM BREWING COMPANY

Years in business:	15 (founded in 1991)
Start-up capital:	$60,000
Annual sales (2005):	NA
Corporate form:	Private for-profit (S corporation)
Business:	Artisan beers

■ ■

As impressive as those business results are, the firm's social and environmental accomplishments are equally profound:

- Employee ownership through an ESOP (employee stock ownership program) now controls 32 percent of the business.
- Open-book management, backed by training, gives every employee access to all of the firm's financial and planning data except salaries.
- A corporate philanthropy program donates $1 for every barrel sold to charities in the states where New Belgium brands are sold.
- A wind-energy program supplies 100 percent of the brewery's electricity requirements.
- A water-conservation program cuts in half the industry average of the amount of water required to brew a barrel of beer.
- State-of-the-art sustainability programs run throughout the entire operation—including green-building specifications, on-site water treatment, methane gas recapture, reuse of spent grains, and recycling of practically everything.[13]

These accomplishments are a direct outgrowth of the vision and passion of the firm's founders, Lebesch and Jordan, who were an electrical engineer and a social worker before they became brew masters. Their vision, "to operate a profitable company that makes our love and talent manifest,"[14] has been embedded in the company's design from the beginning. As CEO Jordan told the 2003 national Craft Brewer's Conference in a keynote address:

Before my husband Jeff and I ever made a barrel of beer, we dreamed about what we wanted New Belgium to be. In 1991, we went on a hike in Rocky Mountain National Park. We took our notebooks along and we sat down on some boulders to talk about what was important to us in starting a brewery. We weren't thinking then about the kind of legacy our vision for New Belgium would produce, we were thinking about what kind of company we would have as we sold 90 cases a week out of our basement. Here were the core values and beliefs that we crafted on that hike:

- We would make world class beers, especially focused on Belgian styles.
- We would be environmental stewards.
- We would promote beer culture.
- We would have fun.

Twelve years later, this vision continues to guide our business.[15]

On the continuum of the difficulty of maintaining a mission focus, illustrated in the figure at the beginning of this chapter, I placed New Belgium Brewing Company in the middle. I suspect this placement would surprise the firm's founders, who have clearly built their entire business around their values. What makes this case different to me is the weaker link between the values of the founders and the values of the brand—that is, the extent to which their customers are buying New Belgium beers because of the firm's social and environmental commitments versus other values, like the flavor of the beer.

This is by no means intended as a criticism. In fact, it's quite the opposite: I'm suggesting that Jordan and Lebesch have chosen to do the right thing in their business simply because they believe it is the right thing to do—regardless of the impact on the firm's market or financial performance. Some of their values-based decisions, like the decision to do on-site wastewater treatment, have clear bottom-line benefits; others, like their decision to meet 100 percent of their brewery's power requirements through wind energy, have an adverse impact on the bottom line.

Despite their location in the middle of the continuum, at least three factors make their mission commitments easier to maintain: (1) they have no outside investors, (2) they are able to charge a premium for their product, and (3) as owners, they are unambiguously committed to living their values in their work.

Tweezerman International

One step farther in degree of difficulty on the continuum is Tweezerman, a company that Dal LaMagna founded in 1980 to serve as an example of his vision of "responsible capitalism." Tweezerman, which LaMagna sold in 2004 to German-based Zwilling J. A. Henckels, is the world's premier provider of "personal-care products"—tweezers, nail clippers, eyelash curlers, nose-hair trimmers, and the like.

■ ■

TWEEZERMAN INTERNATIONAL

Years in business:	26 (founded in 1980)
Start-up capital:	$500
Annual sales (2005):	$35 million
Corporate form:	Private for-profit
Business:	Personal-care products

■ ■

As with New Belgium, the values of the company may not be intrinsic to the brand, but they are definitely intrinsic to the man behind the brand. As LaMagna tells the story:

I had wanted to be in public service, so I thought I would do what Voltaire had done, make myself a million bucks and then be able to commit myself to be in politics without being subservient to political party or moneyed interests.

So I set out to be successful in business. Well, I failed at practically everything you could possibly imagine. I had four,
five, six ventures that flopped. And then I went to the Harvard Business School. I got in probably because they read
my résumé and they felt I was somebody they could help,
and by the time I got out . . . I was $150,000 in debt and still
frustrated in my attempt to be successful. In fact, about 10
years after my graduation from the Harvard Business School
one of my classmates had figured out that I had caused the
class average to drop by $80 because I'd made so little
money that year. I was 32 then. I was still a failure.

So I kind of left and I was out in Hollywood back then, trying to be a movie producer. And for me it was either be a
movie producer and make movies to change the world, or
be a political person and change the world through politics. That's where I was at. So I left, came back home, lived
with my mother and sister, got on my sister's bike, and
found a job. The only job I'd ever had in my life. And after
a year I found myself selling tweezers. . . .

At that point I decided, because I really wasn't into being
a business person, I was interested more in creating a business model that the world could embrace that was one that
just didn't exploit everything in its sight. And that's what I
had in my heart. For instance, I started Tweezerman and as
soon as possible I provided health insurance to my employees. . . . I always thought of my employees as the most important thing to my business enterprise. The product was
second. The customers were third. Seems backwards but
that's the way I operated.[16]

That commitment to employees is the thing that stands out
again and again in the Tweezerman story. When LaMagna was
the owner, the firm offered *all* of its employees a full comple-
ment of core employee benefits—profit sharing, stock ownership, a 401(k) plan, health insurance, company-paid training
and education courses, and a variety of on-site services, from

yoga classes and massages to dry cleaning and English-language instruction for nonnative speakers. But the company went even further in its commitment to providing a "living wage" to all entry-level hourly workers, and to maintaining a zero-layoff policy even in times of economic distress. Tweezerman was cited in an *Inc.* magazine article for keeping its workforce intact despite a 25 percent downturn in sales in the wake of September 11.

> LaMagna first froze hiring, even for replacements at the company's headquarters and at its remanufacturing facility, in Houston. When people left, their responsibilities were distributed among the remaining staff. Cross-training became the norm: pickers also became packagers, and shippers checked accounts. The director of product development volunteered to work three days instead of five at a prorated salary, and other executives offered to follow suit as needed. To avoid layoffs at the remanufacturing plant (where 10% of the product mix originated), LaMagna continued to import raw materials, such as unfinished cuticle-nipper forgings from India, even though that meant stocking up on inventory.
>
> Then came the hardest part: freezing wages and salaries. Typically, Tweezerman budgets 20% of its sales for employee wages, salaries, and benefits. As sales dropped, that ratio got out of kilter, with about 25% of sales going to the compensation pool. To bring about a balance, LaMagna first suspended his own salary for the last two months of 2001 and cut it by 60% for 2002. He then put the money that the company was saving from lowered interest rates on its bank loans into the compensation pot instead of into profits or new investments. If by the end of fiscal 2002 sales have outstripped the cutbacks in compensation, LaMagna will distribute the difference as retroactive raises. "It's a good-faith agreement with everyone," he says.[17]

LaMagna continued to keep the faith with his employees right through the sale of the company. He chose his buyer—a privately held, employee-friendly company founded in 1731 (yes, *1*731!)—very carefully, and insisted upon three conditions that would preserve the Tweezerman legacy: the company would remain in Port Washington, New York; no employees, including members of the management team, would lose their jobs as a result of the sale; and the new owners would maintain Tweezerman's commitment to being a socially responsible business. Then LaMagna and the new owners teamed up to pass out $1.8 million in "stay-on" bonuses to employees.[18]

In addition to the conditions ensuring the continuation of his benevolent employment policies, LaMagna's third sale condition ensured the continuation of the company's Second Bottom Line programs—that is, its philanthropic initiatives. In La-Magna's 24 years with the company, those gifts represented 5 percent of annual profits and included major contributions in the areas of health, community, environment, and youth; company matches of up to $500 per employee to an even broader range of charities; and a variety of company-backed employee volunteer efforts.

All of these practices were purely voluntary—things that La-Magna chose to do to prove the viability of his unique brand of socially responsible business. And in the end he feels that his choices definitely paid off.

The reason I was able to grow . . . to be successful . . . to build such a strong brand . . . to sell for so much at the end, was because of this symphony of practices that sang, that played the song of responsible capitalism.

Anybody involved in Tweezerman loved the product, loved the way we did business with them, and loved the people they dealt with. That whole thing ends up being a different way of acting as a capitalist, which is kind of the old-fashioned way. It pays off—the company works. I had less stress, I had a more enjoyable life, and everybody involved with me, all of my employees, had a better life and as a result were more productive.

So, sure, you can underpay your employees by 5 percent, and if you're a $100 million company, that means your shareholders are making an extra $5 million, or $2.5 million, or whatever it is, based on the cost of sales. But if you did that, I would argue that in the long run you would shoot yourself in the foot, and you wouldn't have something that has value. There's more to life than an extra dollar. It's how you feel, the amount of stress that you have, how you are received by other people in the world, how you're respected, all that stuff.[19]

Like New Belgium, Tweezerman had the advantage of growing without taking on significant outside investment,[20] the ability to charge a premium for its products, and an owner unambiguously committed to building a business based on his values. I placed Tweezerman one step farther to the right on the continuum of difficulty for two reasons: (1) it seems a heck of a lot harder to build a premium position for a pair of tweezers than for an artisan beer, and (2) LaMagna appears to have successfully managed the ultimate challenge for mission-driven entrepreneurs, having negotiated the transfer of his values with the transfer of his business to new ownership (as you'll see in Chapter 4).

Wild Planet Toys Inc.

The final company profiled in this chapter faced a set of industry dynamics that were an order of magnitude more difficult than any of the others. In the toy business, while the product may be about fun, the competitive environment is anything but.

Nonetheless, for Danny Grossman, the founder of Wild Planet Toys, the passion was toys and the vision was "to create quality products that spark the imagination and provide positive play experiences for children."[21] The company has done that suc-

cessfully since 1993, earning many industry and community service awards along the way.

▪ ▪

WILD PLANET TOYS INC.

Years in business:	13 (founded in 1993)
Start-up capital:	NA
Annual sales (2005):	NA
Corporate form:	Private for-profit
Business:	Toys

▪ ▪

The original idea behind the company was "No guns, no Barbies"—that is, Wild Planet would make toys that were nonvio-
lent and gender neutral.[22] That has proved to be easier said than
done. According to Jennifer Chapman, the company's COO,

> The mission has morphed over the years as we've grown up.
> When the company was founded, no one in the company
> had kids. So the idea of gender neutral made sense to them.
> And then come to find out two things: that the toy industry
> is completely organized around gender, and that girls and
> boys play very differently. So the first go-round was to say
> toys that don't rely on gender stereotypes, and then the cur-
> rent wording is toys that respect girls and boys. And we've
> come to see both the differences in play patterns and also
> see how difficult that idea of gender neutral is to play out in
> the marketplace.
>
> We have a child psychologist who works for the company,
> helps us with our research, and also challenges us [with]
> philosophical questions, the values questions, discussions
> about what kind of products we're looking at making. And
> the conversation we've been having lately is about aggres-
> sion versus violence.
>
> We're kind of dancing up to the line. We haven't made any
> guns. We made a water launcher that launched water balls.

This spring we have a line called Battle Crawlers, and they're bugs that fight with one another. And our research showed that video games and TV and movies are incredibly influential when it comes to actually impacting kids' behavior, as distinct from role playing with other creatures, things, etc., to sort of get out aggression, which is different from violence.

These are the kinds of conversations we have as we're thinking of products. We make our decisions, and sometimes not everyone in the company totally supports the decision. We welcome questions and dialogue about what we're doing, which is important to us as far as being a values-based company.[23]

Of all the industries I looked at, the toy business was one of the toughest in terms of market pressures, which made the accomplishments of Wild Planet that much more impressive. The company maintains its commitment to sparking the imagination of children through the "open-ended" toys it creates, the quarterly Toy Opinion Parties it hosts with young customers, the creative work its employees do with kids from low-income families through its Invention Invasion program, and the annual Kid Inventor Challenge it sponsors. The winning entry in that competition is manufactured and sold as a Wild Planet toy, with royalties going to its inventor.[24]

Wild Planet also maintains a strong commitment to its 50-plus U.S. employees and the workforce employed by its manufacturing contractors in China. It has offered pioneering employee benefits in the areas of family and paid time for volunteer efforts in the community. Like New Belgium Brewing Company, Wild Planet maintains an open set of books. All of its employees have health insurance, stock options, and "access to a channel of dissent." More important, all of its employees can participate in the lively, ongoing internal conversations about what the company is doing—and what it should be doing.[25]

Beyond the firm's San Francisco headquarters, Wild Planet is also concerned about the treatment of employees in the Chinese factories where its toys are made. The firm pays "two to three times the provincial going rate" and has its factories inspected weekly,[26] but its real work on the labor issue has been through the Toy Industry Association (TIA). CEO Danny Grossman, who was a foreign diplomat and human rights observer before founding Wild Planet, has put his energy into the TIA board and an effort to shape international labor standards at the industry level—a high-leverage strategy for a relatively small player in an industry dominated by giants.

What is most unusual about Wild Planet Toys is its decision to compete with the giants in the mainstream toy business. Life would have been a lot easier for the company if it had simply chosen to go after a niche in the specialty toy business. But, as Chapman pointed out,

> From the beginning, we also knew that we wanted to reach a wide variety of kids in terms of economic and class backgrounds. So we never said, "We're going to be the mom-and-pop company," or, "We're going to make our toys out of recycled goods." We were clear that to play the game the way the game was played, we would need to be price-competitive, manufactured in China, etc. [Growth] is important to us because we believe in what we're doing, and to the degree that we can own more of the marketplace, we're able to reach more kids, and that's what we want to do.[27]

In terms of the continuum that started this chapter, Wild Planet Toys has the hardest row to hoe. At present, the mainstream industry in which the firm has chosen to compete offers no premium for the mission that animates the founder and the firm. If anything, the industry is actively hostile to Wild Planet's "No guns, no Barbies" values. And the price competition that dominates the toy business hardly supports exceptional employee benefits in the United States or livable wages for overseas producers. Finally, the toy business is capital intensive—not from a manufacturing perspective (manufacturing can be contracted to others) but from a marketing perspective. As a consequence, Wild Planet Toys has outside investors who create pressures on mission that none of the other companies profiled in this chapter had to face.

While all these issues make Wild Planet Toys' accomplishments especially impressive, they also suggest at least a couple of factors that make mission-driven business more difficult in some industries than in others. Things to avoid: intense competition based on price that squeezes margins to the point where there's no money left for social values, and capital-intensive business strategies that require significant outside investment and dilute the founder's control.

■■LESSONS LEARNED

The most striking thing to me about this collection of examples is their variety: different industries, different strategies, different value propositions, different capital requirements, and different organizational structures.

But in all cases, I think it's safe to say that mission came first and business came second—just as we noted in the previous chapter. The purpose of each business was to allow its founders to live their values at work. This is very different from the founding stories of most businesses, which tend to focus on seeing an underdeveloped opportunity in the marketplace—and building a business to make money by addressing that opportunity. The mission statements of most companies focus on service to customers as the highest organizational value; the companies profiled in this book tended to have a broader social mission, at least part of which was to create a new business model as an example to others.

A second thing that struck me was the importance each of these entrepreneurs placed on treating employees well. This might seem to be a no-brainer for a mission-driven firm, but it is far from obvious—and is quite distinct from the pattern of many conventional start-ups, mission-driven nonprofits, and an earlier generation of mission-driven businesses. It has not been uncommon for organizations in those categories to exploit their labor forces by offering lower wages or benefits or requiring longer hours in exchange for the satisfaction of more meaningful work. The companies profiled in this chapter have not done that. They've stressed the importance of compensation, job security, employee ownership, profit sharing, and open-book management. In all cases, they've reaped the benefits of employee loyalty—higher quality, lower turnover—but that has not appeared to be their motivation. Doing the right thing—and walking the talk—have been the more important drivers.

The third lesson I took from these stories was the desirability of building the values of the company into the fabric of the business and, whenever possible, into the value of the brand. If the values of the business are an afterthought, or a nice-to-have, or a pet project of the founder's, they are too easily set aside when times get tough or the business is sold. It is interesting to see the variety of ways in which values were embedded into the core businesses of these firms. At the New Belgium Brewing Company, the environmental commitments were built into the company's core capital assets. At Wild Planet Toys, the core values are expressed through the products the company brings to market. At Tweezerman, maintenance of the company's core values was written into the company sale agreement. At Novex Couriers, a large part of the brand identity has been built around the Novex Clean platform, including its highly visible hybrid vehicles. At Village Real Estate Services, the entire focus of the enterprise, in both its for-profit and nonprofit arms, is on supporting a vision of a vibrant urban community.

No business is easy, but some businesses are harder than others. The same is true of mission-driven businesses: some businesses—and ways of doing business—make it easier to maintain a commitment to mission. But any business—or at least many businesses—*can* do it even as they go to scale. And that is a vision worth hanging on to. ■■

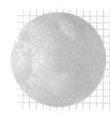

CHAPTER THREE

Organic Is the Way to Grow

WHEN IT COMES TO THINKING about how to grow a business, I have a double learning disability: an MBA from Stanford and about 10 years of working in the computer software industry. Both of those experiences give me a distorted view of reality: too much emphasis on outside investors; too much concern about first-mover advantage and early market share; too much pressure to "get big fast."[1]

I mention my biases here because I think they may be fairly widespread. To some extent, we are still suffering from a collective dot-com hangover, which is really only the latest—and perhaps most extreme—version of the all-American, *Inc.* 500, fast-growth success story. A handful of the companies I interviewed for this book grew really rapidly (and made the *Inc.* 500)—but *only* a handful. The predominant growth story was slow and "organic"—a natural unfolding of the business, a one-thing-leads-to-another approach.

This approach *does* scale. It just scales a little more slowly than the venture capital model that has created such high expectations in the public imagination. But in fact most businesses of all sorts—mission driven or not—grow more slowly than that. And just because a business grows more slowly and organically does not mean it cannot eventually become quite large.

Organic Valley Family of Farms

Organic Valley Family of Farms is a perfect case in point. Founded in a Wisconsin barn in 1988 by seven family farmers, the business has grown—organically—to a $245 million cooperative selling 200 branded products produced by 723 organic farmers to customers in all 50 states, most of Canada, and parts of Japan.[2]

▪ ▪

ORGANIC VALLEY FAMILY OF FARMS

Years in business:	18 (founded in 1988)
Start-up capital:	Less than $1,000
Annual sales (2005):	$245 million
Corporate form:	Agricultural cooperative
Business:	Organic food

▪ ▪

Arguably, the single most important thing to understand about Organic Valley is its organizational form as a farmer-owned cooperative. Everything else flows from that central fact. As the organization's Web site says,

Part of our success is due to the fact that as farmer-owners, we pay ourselves a stable, equitable and sustainable price. In an era of rising and falling agricultural prices, the family farmers who produce our organic milk, juice, eggs, meat, and produce can rely on a stable, living wage to stay in business in their home regions. . . . Being farmer-owned and independent has also allowed us to stay true to our mission—keeping family farmers farming.[3]

Organic Valley was born in an effort to preserve family farms by stabilizing dairy prices. As nonorganic agriculture moved in the direction of agribusiness—toward larger and larger, more chemically intensive corporate farms—a significant portion of the American consumer market moved in the opposite direction. The grocery marketplace overall grew at about 2 percent a year, but the market for organic foods grew at about 20 percent.[4]

With the wind of that market trend filling its sails (and fueling its sales), Organic Valley developed a hybrid local-regional-national strategy that enabled it to get to scale while supporting its core constituency of small family farms. At the local level, Organic Valley was able to promise its producers a stable price that would make their operations sustainable at a family-farm scale. At the regional level, the co-op was large enough to strike distribution and processing deals that would fill up the facilities of its "co-pack" processing partners, allowing it to avoid building production facilities of its own. To this day, the co-op itself owns only two processing facilities, while marketing over 500 different products manufactured in 65 contracted processing plants.[5] At the national level, the co-op manages the Organic Valley Family of Farms brand, which sells throughout the country.

According to Organic Valley founder and C-E-I-E-I-O[6] George Siemon,

> We really believe in local, but we've had to become national in order to become real in the marketplace and to have the influence that the farmers wanted. So we are trying to satisfy that local market by having a local milk that's made in the region. The farmers believe in it—they have a lot of pride in that. As well as the consumer—they're concerned about the local, they're concerned about the family farms.
>
> But our butters and cheeses are not local. If the market grows big enough, we'll make everything in regions. Right now the market is only so big, and milk is the big driver, so milk is where we're able to do local. We have milk in 14 different states now, and we've got eggs in five states and we're going to expand that to where we have eggs all around the country, just like the milk. So we are following up this national scale, local flavor of regional products.[7]

Although the growth of Organic Valley has been anything but slow—averaging 22 percent a year over the first 18 years of its existence[8]—it has been organic in some respects. The real driver of the co-op's growth has been the underlying growth in consumer demand for organic products. Organic Valley has responded to that trend by building a brand and the infrastructure to support it. Money has been tight throughout the organization's history—co-ops have a notoriously hard time securing outside funding—which has led the group to be conservative in its capital spending. It has not had to grow to satisfy investor expectations or to fill up excess plant capacity. It has only had to grow to satisfy customer demand and, more important, to meet the needs of its farmer-producers.

The real bottom line for Organic Valley is not the actual profit of the business, but rather the price differential between what its member farms would receive selling their products through conventional channels and what they receive as a premium for participating in the Organic Valley brand. The average dairy premium was $3.50/cwt (hundredweight) for the first five years, $4.50/cwt for the next seven years, and $6.50 for the past five years, and it looks as if it will jump to $9/cwt going forward.[9] That's enough of a difference to create a future in a field that was dying at a rate of 219 farms per day.[10]

Birkenstock USA

At Birkenstock, growth was both slow and organic. As Margot Fraser, the legendary founder and CEO, put it:

> It's really more that the enterprise itself grew. It was more like you put a seed in the ground and it starts growing. There wasn't a plan, let's do this, that, and the other to make it grow.[11]

She started Birkenstock Footprint Sandals in 1966 as a very low-key import business, purchasing 6 to 12 pairs at a time and selling them out of her home in Santa Cruz, California. She was totally sold on the comfort of the shoes' unique contoured cork footbed, which she had discovered while traveling in Europe and looking for relief from her own chronic foot pain. When she attempted to sell the shoes to conventional shoe retailers, she was told, "Women will never wear those shoes." Nonetheless, she persevered and eventually found a market in the nascent health-foods movement.[12]

■ ■

Birkenstock USA

Years in business:	40 (founded in 1966)
Start-up capital:	NA
Annual sales (2005):	NA
Corporate form:	Employee-owned for-profit
Business:	Footwear

■ ■

Six years later, she formally ramped up the business with a $6,000 bank loan secured by San Rafael health-food-store owner June Embury, her first and best customer. Once Fraser had a few hard orders, she borrowed money from the bank—on Embury's credit, since she, as a single woman, otherwise would not have been able to obtain bank financing. "At that time, a single woman couldn't even get credit to buy gasoline. I had to team up with my married friend to borrow money." With no business plan or sales forecast, the pair earned $125,000 in revenue the first year—and the business was off and running.[13]

It wasn't incorporated, however, as Birkenstock Footprint Sandals, an entity separate from the German firm actually manufacturing the shoes, until 1982. At that point, the droll Fraser recalled,

Our customers were young people who were anti-establishment, and who didn't want to look like their mothers. But many of them were living with their mothers, and soon their mothers said, "I'd like to be comfortable, too," and they bought Birkenstocks. It was a "trickle up" effect.[14]

Through most of its history, the company grew slowly, a situation that suited Fraser perfectly. Since she had no formal business background, it gave her a chance to develop her own business skills and those of the people who worked with her. It also allowed her to maintain financial control of the company, which gave her the freedom to run it according to her values and beliefs. Some of her most deeply held beliefs involved people—treating people well, helping them to develop their potential, involving them in company decision making, promoting from within, and ultimately giving employees ownership of the company.[15] Employees had started with 10 percent ownership in the company's early days, but in 1997 she sold another 30 percent to her employees, and in 2002 she sold the remainder to the employee stock ownership program (ESOP).

Unfortunately, by December 2004 she was back in the role of CEO, and in the spring of 2005, when I spoke with her, she was fighting for the company's life. Numerous issues had contributed to Birkenstock's woes: a terrible exchange rate that necessitated problematic price increases, difficulties in the relationship with the Birkenstock factory in Germany, significant competition from Birkenstock knockoffs, the launch of a new line of footwear that didn't go as well as planned, and so on.[16] Directly or indirectly, all of these were management problems that stemmed from an imperfect changing of the guard from Fraser to the ESOP management team—and the change from an organic growth model to something more targeted. Fraser observed,

> I found over the years that planning is wonderful as an exercise. But you have to be flexible because reality is usually different, and suddenly you grow from an area in the business that you might have even neglected. But you have to be alert to noticing what wants to happen and what is feasible.

And it may be, the people that came after me didn't quite notice that and were more into, "Let's plan goals where it's supposed to come from and then execute it." . . . I think that it's very important that management does not just have ideas and great visions. The business fundamentals have to be there to make it.[17]

By July 2005, Fraser was back in retirement, having handed over the reins to Gene Kunde, the organization's COO, who now serves as president and CEO. He moved quickly to refocus the company on its core business, the Birkenstock product line, partly by shedding five other labels the company had taken on in recent years.[18] It was back to basics and a more organic approach to growth.

Seventh Generation Inc.

The third example of the case for organic growth is another founder-led firm that grew—this one by fits and starts—to a significant national brand. Like Organic Valley, Seventh Generation got its start in a business adjacent to the one where it finally caught hold. The original business, in which Jeffrey Hollender acquired a 50 percent stake in 1989, was a mail-order catalog of natural products called Renew America.

■ ■

SEVENTH GENERATION INC.

Years in business:	17 (Hollender acquired a 50 percent stake in the Renew America catalog business in 1989)
Start-up capital:	NA
Annual sales (2005):	NA
Corporate form:	Private for-profit
Business:	Household products

■ ■

The mail-order business was a roller-coaster ride for the next six years, and Hollender eventually sold off the catalog in order to be able to concentrate on building his retail brand. This he did incrementally, moving from mail order to natural-foods retail to mainstream retail; from toilet paper to a full line of household paper and cleaning products; from a regional focus to a national brand.

It absolutely took time, and it was the result of endless persistence. There was no single breakthrough mode. We are very much a sales- and market-oriented company, and we drove ourselves to scale through sales and marketing, and then brought the rest of our business along the path as the sales grew.

And the fact that it is incremental presents both opportunities and challenges. If everything changes overnight, you know that everything has changed overnight and you've got to reevaluate. If things change incrementally, you have to know when to change different parts of your business that are no longer functioning the way they need to function. That is in part helped by creating a culture that has an openness and honesty so people can safely communicate how they feel, because in many cases it was not me who saw the need to change.[19]

The issue of scale has affected Seventh Generation in every area of its business, from manufacturing to supply-chain management to sales and marketing and distribution, and Hollender was particularly articulate in describing its impacts.

Scale affects every aspect of our business. If you look at just manufacturing, making basic consumer products, there are huge issues relative to scale and volume—whether it's buying raw materials or being able to run in factories that have technologies that allow us to achieve the highest quality at the lowest price. For many years, we were nowhere near the kind of scale that could allow us the gross margins we needed to make a profit . . . and that was in large part because the manufacturing was so inefficient. As we grew larger, we saw dramatic reductions in our cost of goods and significant improvements in the quality that we were able to purchase. That's most true of making paper products, and it's less true of making cleaning products, [which] tend to be made efficiently at a smaller scale.

So one thing that you have to understand when you start a business is, if you're selling a product, what are those scale issues? What advantage is someone going to have just because they're larger than you are? If Procter & Gamble has six warehouses and six manufacturing facilities around the country and I've got two, there is no way that I'm going to be able to manage my operations and logistics as cost-effectively, because I've got to ship everything farther than they do to get to the marketplace.

So you have significant scale issues in operations and distribution, and certainly when it comes to sales and marketing. It was only two or three years ago that we started to advertise. We never had done traditional consumer advertising, because we simply didn't have the money to be able to afford to do it effectively. And when you're small, it's hard to attract the attention of the best sales brokers because they know that they're not going to make a lot of money selling your product. As you get bigger and you're able to generate bigger commission checks, you can get a higher-quality broker.

To a large extent, we faced some of those [same] challenges internally. We hired a human resources person 2½ years ago. As important as that aspect of our business was, we just didn't justify spending the money to have a full-time person until [then]. And that goes to the heart also of the issue of pace. One of the things that I had to come to realize is, while there are a hundred things I would like to do, I have to be very clear about what the most important ones are and understand the fifth year, maybe I could take five things off that list and do them, and next year I can take another five, but I will end up out of business if I try to take all hundred at the same time.

Those issues apply as much to your values and expression of your values as they do to other aspects of your business. Some things—honesty and integrity—are nonnegotiable and have nothing to do with scale. And I think you differentiate the nonnegotiable aspects of your values and your culture as a company from the aspects of your values that are related to scale.

A good example of values related to scale is in terms of the influence that we can have over our supply chain and our manufacturers. There is no question that as you get bigger, you command greater influence. If five years ago I would have asked some of my suppliers whether they were giving health insurance to their factory workers, they probably would have laughed at me. Today, I am able to establish guidelines throughout my supply chain that those suppliers will have to have. You can't end up feeling guilty because you can't do all of those things at once, but you do need to be transparent about it.

So today, obviously, there are still hundreds of things that Seventh Generation isn't doing that I would like to do, that I will grow into over time. What's important is to be open and honest and transparent about what you are doing and what you're not doing.[20]

■■LESSONS LEARNED

My take-away from these three examples and the other stories I heard was that a slower, more organic growth pattern has tremendous advantages for mission-driven firms. It reduces their reliance upon outside investors and thereby enables them to maintain their commitment to mission. Its pace allows people— including the founder-CEOs—to grow into their jobs and pursue their visions over time. Its pace better allows employees to maintain their health and well-being, and the company is better able to maintain its corporate culture.

It is not, however, slow.

It is simply slower. The three businesses profiled here share several attributes that made their organic growth possible. First, they let someone else do their manufacturing. As a consequence, they didn't have to make a huge capital investment and then drive their growth to fill the plant. They left that problem to their manufacturing partners: Birkenstock's German manufacturer; Organic Valley's co-pack firms; Seventh Generation's contracted manufacturing facilities.

Second, they essentially followed market demand, rather than making huge investments to create it. They tapped into an underlying market trend and rode that wave to success. In the United States, there is a long-term trend of growing concern for human health that has kept the organic-foods sector, for example, growing at 20 percent per year since 1990.[21] All three of the businesses profiled in this chapter were able to tap into this trend[22] and use the sector's growth as the engine for their own growth.

Third, each business developed a unique value proposition that kept competitors at bay long enough for them to establish the premier position within their segment. All three now have significant competition, but each was able to firmly establish its brand within its niche before it attracted strong competitors. As their niches broadened and went mainstream, each of these companies enjoyed the position of being the flagship brand within its category. For Organic Valley and Seventh Generation, which had managed to control their manufacturing costs, this translated into strong growth in both sales and profits. For Birkenstock, with high manufacturing costs from the sole-source agreement with its eponymous German supplier, profits have been more elusive.

If those are some of the advantages of organic growth, what are the disadvantages—and when is organic *not* the way to grow? The answers are related. When a market is growing rapidly and attracting significant competition (in terms of either numbers or clout), organic growth may not be fast enough to maintain a presence in the emerging market. You need to either meet the challenge by expanding more rapidly, or plan to settle into a niche or a series of niches.

Organic growth is also problematic in situations involving classic economies of scale, where you are required to make significant investments—in either marketing or manufacturing—ahead of demand. As you will see in subsequent chapters, that usually means bringing in outside money, which means delivering an "acceptable" return on investment in a "reasonable" amount of time—all of which places you on your investors' timetable rather than your own and may make organic growth impossible. Investor-driven growth also makes it considerably more difficult to manage to your mission, as we'll see in the next chapter. ■ ■

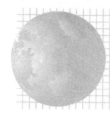

CHAPTER FOUR

Finance Your Independence

By NOW, virtually every mission-driven entrepreneur knows the sad ending to the tale of Ben & Jerry's: the forced sale of one of the country's premier socially responsible businesses to a giant multinational clearly focused on the financial bottom line.

Ben Cohen and Jerry Greenfield actually made their fatal mistake 16 years before the company's sale to Unilever, when they decided to raise capital by selling shares of stock to their loyal Vermont customers. From there, it was only a matter of time before the shares appreciated in value, began to be traded for their financial return rather than their social cachet, and ultimately fell into the hands of institutional investors who thought an offer of $43.60 a share without Ben and Jerry was more attractive than an offer of $38 a share with them.

The obvious lesson from the Ben & Jerry's story was this: whatever you do, don't go public! But the deeper question was both less obvious and more pervasive: how do you raise enough capital to grow your business without losing control?

Arguably, this is *the* critical issue that this book must address. It is a critical issue for all entrepreneurs, but it is doubly difficult and important for entrepreneurs who choose to pursue both mission and money. Conventional investors are not used to evaluating investments that seek social returns as well as financial returns, and they *assume*—sometimes rightly and sometimes not—that such investments yield lower returns. There are groups of investors, such as the members of Investors' Circle,[1] that actively pursue investments because of their social returns,

but most mainstream investors are more than a little wary of dou-
ble- and triple-bottom-line businesses that seek something more
than a financial return. And without access to capital, it's virtually impossible to scale.

A quick preview of the financial lessons to come:

- Bootstrap, bootstrap, bootstrap.
- Use debt rather than equity.
- Choose your investors carefully—and meet them on their
  own terms.
- Build mission into your value proposition.
- Invent new instruments.
- Exit with care.

■ ■ Bootstrap, bootstrap, bootstrap

Businesses typically begin as ideas, grow into obsessions, and
eventually begin to consume significant amounts of cash. All of
this can occur before they ever encounter their first customer—
much less their first breakeven month.

Contrary to the illusion created during the dot-com era, most
businesses finance their start-up requirements through some
form of *bootstrapping*—that is, using cleverness and cash-conser-
vation strategies to get to the point where sales begin to cover
expenses and support modest growth. This gives them the freedom to make their own business decisions (and mistakes) without having to worry about the financial requirements of outside
investors. Bootstrapping has the further advantage of fostering
the kinds of business discipline—frugality, hard work, focus,
accountability—required to successfully create something out of
nothing. It also tends to support the kind of slower, more
organic growth discussed in the last chapter, giving entrepreneurs a chance to grow their management skills at a pace com-
mensurate with the natural growth rate of the business.

Here is a list of some of the most commonly used bootstrapping resources.

Sources of Bootstrap Capital

Personal Resources

Motivation: Desire to see the enterprise succeed.

- "Sweat equity": working for nothing in the present in the hope of creating value in the future through one's ownership of the business (sometimes financed by one's "day job" or one's spouse's job).
- Work for reduced or deferred compensation.
- Personal savings.
- Credit card debt.
- Second mortgage or home equity line of credit.

Resources from Employees

Motivation: Desire to earn a significant amount of money and a preferred position in the organization if it is successful.

- "Sweat equity": being paid in stock rather than in (or in addition to) wages.
- Work for reduced or deferred compensation.
- Work as freelancers, contractors, or short-term or part-time employees.

Resources from Customers

Motivation: Desire to purchase the product and ensure its availability.

- Development contracts to cover R & D expenses.
- Prepaid licenses, royalties, or advances (usually at a discounted rate).
- Prompt payment of invoices (supported with discount incentives).
- Special deals, including barter, for use of customer facilities or equipment.

Resources from Suppliers

Motivation: Desire to secure a long-term customer relationship.

- Trade credit and generous payment terms (sometimes offered by the supplier and sometimes simply taken by the entrepreneur as late payments).

- Buy on consignment.
- Barter.
- Special deals for use of facilities, equipment, or staff resources.
- Special deals with suppliers of professional services.

Resources from Savings on Operations

Motivation: "Easy money" totally within the founder's control.

- Cultivate a personal reputation as a tightwad—that is, being frugal in your use of company resources. Deserve your reputation!
- Cultivate a company culture of frugality.
- Start small and cheap to generate cash that will enable you to grow.
- Work from home, in subleased or shared facilities, or in other low-rent space.
- Lease equipment instead of buying it.
- Focus on short-term cash management rather than on other longer-term business goals.
- Keep good records and manage your business professionally to establish a track record for future outside funding.

Kim Jordan and Jeff Lebesch, of New Belgium Brewing Company, bootstrapped their operation from nothing to a 31,000-barrels-a-year operation before they got their first bank financing. The couple started the business in the basement of their house in 1991.

> We were there for about a year and a half, and we ended up having more square footage in beer than we did in furniture, and a garage that had a walk-in cooler in it and storage space for empty glasses. We decided it was time to do something new, so we moved to our second location.
>
> On the initial capital, we were very sophisticated and took a second mortgage out on our house, which I'm sure is a common story. And we used our credit cards—all of those, "You have been pre-approved for a line of credit." Plus we

both had jobs. So we felt like, you know, we'd take a second mortgage out and if this business didn't work, we'd go back to real jobs.

Probably our most interesting financing was actually before we moved into our second location. We were in that awkward stage where we weren't yet on the bank's radar. We presold our existing equipment to a guy with a 10 percent discount and a promise to train him on how to use it if he would let us keep the equipment for four months. So we used that money as the down payment on our new equipment. And we told our new equipment manufacturers that whoever could arrange for an operating lease would get the business. So one of the manufacturers found a leasing company to work with us. We borrowed money from my mom and dad; we lived on our credit cards again. So that's how we funded our second location and our first big expansion.

And by then we were on the bank's radar, and we've [now] actually gotten to the point where we're a fairly significant customer for Wells Fargo.[2]

▨▨ Use debt rather than equity

When people decry the shortage of capital available for mission-driven firms, they are generally talking about the lack of equity capital. The situation with debt is a little bit different, and it's worth noting the differences between the two.

Equity capital is money at risk. In general, it is placed at risk in the hope of a higher return—and in exchange for an ownership stake in the business. Both of those conditions can be problematic for mission-driven entrepreneurs. First, the returns may be lower or slower than the returns from competing investment opportunities. Second, the ability to maintain the commitment to mission requires a certain level of owner control, which founders are understandably reluctant to cede to outside investors. Third, the typical equity investor requires an exit strategy—that is, some sort of "liquidity event" that will enable him/her to convert equity ownership into cash. The investors' desire for liquidity has caused many an owner to sell before he or she was ready—and without adequate mechanisms in place to preserve the commitment to mission.

Debt, on the other hand, looks roughly the same to mission-driven entrepreneurs as to their financially driven counterparts. Debt is secured, either by the assets of the business or by some other set of assets (such as the entrepreneur's house). As long as the ownership structure is relatively standard—which it is *not*, in the case of nonprofit ventures or co-ops—banks basically apply the same criteria to mission-driven businesses as they do to others. Thus, bank loans and lines of credit were important to almost all of the growing businesses I interviewed—they just didn't meet the need for start-up funding, which is where equity typically plays a more important role.

The story of New Belgium Brewing Company is fairly typical. Bankers look for business experience, a track record of success, a strong management team, solid collateral, a proven business model. It has been said that banks lend money only to people who don't really need it—and that's not far from the truth. But once mission-driven businesses become "bankable," they face few if any special obstacles. On the other hand, the worthiness of their goals doesn't entitle them to any special treatment. When it comes to bankers, business is business.

A brief summary of the differences between debt and equity and some of the special considerations for mission-driven firms appear in the table which follows.

The suggestion that mission-driven firms use debt rather than equity to meet their needs for outside capital is not intended to downplay the ability of bankers to exert control over the lives of entrepreneurs. They can easily, and too frequently do, force their customers into liquidation simply by tightening their credit terms. Banking relationships are just that—relationships. As such, they must be cultivated and nurtured—and, given the importance of money to the business, it is helpful to have at least one backup banking prospect in case the primary relationship

Debt	Equity	Mission-driven considerations
Return Fixed according to the terms of the agreement	Variable according to the success of the business	Returns on equity must be competitive with other investments to be attractive to conventional investors. Potential upside is not an issue with debt.
Security Usually secured with collateral	Unsecured	No special considerations unless you have an unusual corporate form, such as nonprofit or cooperative
Repayment Interest usually paid periodically; principal repaid according to terms of the loan	At exit	Exit strategies can be problematic, which is one of the reasons why conventional investors are wary of mission-driven businesses.
Liquidation First in line for repayment if the venture fails	Last in line. Will recover investment (and return) only after all creditors have been paid	No special considerations
Control Exercised through tightening credit terms and availability	Partial ownership with corresponding control, frequently exercised through board participation	Control is an issue for all entrepreneurs, but is especially important to mission-driven entrepreneurs.
Overall Risk (to lender/investor) Relatively low	Relatively high	Because there is less understanding of mission-driven businesses, there is a perception of higher risk among some investors and lenders.

DEBT VS. EQUITY

goes sour. The point of emphasizing debt is simply to recognize that, unlike equity, it is no more problematic for mission-driven firms than it is for other types of businesses.

■■ Choose your investors carefully— and meet them on their own terms

All investors are not created equal. In an ideal world, the mission-driven company would be financed by investors who share the founder's values, time horizon, risk profile, and expectations of an appropriate financial return. There *are* such people, and many can be reached through a handful of networks of socially responsible investors, the most prominent being Investors' Circle.

Since 1992, Investors' Circle has considered 2,400 business concepts and provided an audience for 480 full-scale pitches, and its members have invested over $100 million in 163 companies and small funds. A network of angel investors with a commitment "to galvanize the flow of capital to entrepreneurial companies that enhance bioregional, cultural and economic health and diversity," Investors' Circle focuses on providing "slow money," or "patient capital," to businesses in energy and the environment, food and organics, community and international development, education and media, and health and wellness.[3]

While Investors' Circle is the most well known of the early-stage double-bottom-line investment funds, there are others, many of which are listed in Columbia University's RISE (Research Initiative on Social Enterprise) database and discussed in its 2003 report *RISE Capital Market Report: The Double Bottom Line Private Equity Landscape in 2002/2003*.[4] That study offers a preliminary estimate of the size of the private equity market available to support "double bottom line businesses" (the preferred term of these investors) as between $2 billion and $6 billion[5]—a number that is probably increasing as the renewable-energy sector begins to attract venture capital funds.[6]

While that may sound like a huge amount of money, it represents only about 5 percent of the total venture capital deals concluded during the study period.[7] And the fact remains that very few mission-driven enterprises fit the venture capital model. As Woody Tasch, the chairman of Investors' Circle, observed,

> [V]enture capital typically is invested in companies that are ready to "take off." The analogy of a rocket accelerating to reach escape velocity from the earth's gravitational field has some relevance: Companies that can grow within a few years to billions of dollars of market capitalization and reach the "orbit" of the public marketplace are what drive the 20% return benchmark that is commonly used as the measure of successful venture capital. . . .
>
> [A] venture investment takes years . . . to appreciate. But viewed through the lens of sustainability, through a long-term lens that sees on the horizon population growth, the greenhouse effect, and disequilibria caused by the unprecedented explosion of financial wealth and global consumerism of the last few decades, venture capital is nowhere near patient enough.[8]

Individual investors, assuming you can find them, may have somewhat lower, and slower, expectations. But all investors expect at least a "reasonable" financial return and some sort of an "exit," or way to realize that return through the sale of their interest. Thus, most successful mission-driven entrepreneurs I interviewed had learned how to present their business propositions in conventional investment terms.

Jason Finnis, founder and president of Canada's Hemptown Clothing, is a case in point.[9] He and his girlfriend, Larisa Harrison, started the business—now a $1.3 million apparel manufacturer listed on the OTC Bulletin Board (OTCBB) exchange as HPTWF—with more moxie than money or management expertise. He began the business with $300 when he was a college music major going to flea markets on weekends and exhibiting the wide variety of products that can be made from hemp. After numerous ups and downs, he settled into a niche making hemp T-shirts and selling them in the corporate market.

■ ■

HEMPTOWN CLOTHING

Years in business:	13 (founded in 1993)
Start-up capital:	$300
Annual sales (2005):	$1.33 million
Corporate form:	Public for-profit
Business:	Hemp clothing

■ ■

He and his partner, Jerry Kroll, now the CEO, run the business as a triple-bottom-line company. They tout the environmental benefits of hemp throughout the sales process and are working toward human-rights certification of their manufacturing operations so that they can tout those benefits as part of their pitch to customers to "wear your corporate responsibility on your sleeve."

But when it comes to investors, Finnis is all business. A natural salesman, he has positioned himself to investors as a rabid and unapologetic capitalist.

We're in this to make money; we're a triple-bottom-line company. And as you've seen in our financial statements, we're still working on the most important bottom line, which is profit.[10] We have the environmental and the human-rights [issues] covered, [but] we're not making money. The only way I see green businesses being able to become the standard is if they're just as—if not more—profitable than the traditional businesses.

And that's the thing with green businesses—that we're at an inherent disadvantage from the get-go, because we recognize costs that other business sweep under the rug. [For example], our dyeing process could be a lot cheaper if we didn't pay the surcharge to have [the dye] disposed of responsibly, [or] we didn't worry too much about our use of chlorine. Hydrogen peroxide is more expensive. So we are going to get profitable with the other key parts of our bottom line intact. We're not going to compromise one to be profitable right away.

When we're pitching the company to investors, we're not really talking to them about how environmentally friendly this is. We're talking about market size and how much money we can make them by selling this. We could be selling widgets and we'd probably sell the same pitch. We did the business plan, showed people where we wanted to go, showed them the size of the industry that we're competing in. We drew parallels between the growth of organic food and natural cosmetics, and made that parallel to the textile side. We were able to convince people to invest a fair amount of money.

One of the investors said, "You know what, Jason, you could have Fruit of the Loom or Gildan come and eat your lunch just by adding hemp T-shirts to their product line." And my initial reaction is, "Oh yeah, that would really suck." But when you step back and think of it not as a person who's financially involved in Hemptown, that's the ultimate success—when those big guys start to change the way they're doing their business.[11]

On the other hand, given the fact that Finnis *is* financially involved in Hemptown, he has sought to protect the firm's competitive position by staying a step ahead of the competition. He's expanding his line to include garments made out of bamboo and soy, and has developed a proprietary system for processing hemp, called Crailar®, that may turn out to be the cotton gin of the hemp business.

▪▪Build mission into your value proposition

This is exactly what Jason Finnis and Hemptown have done, and there's a good general principle to be drawn along that line.

Tom McMakin, former chief operating officer of Great Harvest Bread Company and currently a principal in Thrive Capital Partners, a mission-friendly private equity firm, is a great proponent of building corporate values into the brand. In his view, there is a critical distinction between an organization's "commitment to customers and commitment to community." Citing the case of Burt's Bees, a mission-driven natural-products firm that eventually sold to a group of "mainstream investors,"[12] he said:

> [The investors] would never describe themselves in any way as backing socially responsible companies, but here they've got themselves a socially responsible company, so what are they going to do? I think their intention is to keep the commitment going forward insofar as it serves the company's growth.
>
> I really feel like there's a big distinction between commitment to the customer and commitment to the community. Those are two different sorts of social responsibility. When big, strategic buyers that are not mission driven buy these companies, they have to keep the commitment to the customer, but the one that's hard for them to keep is the commitment to the community—to workers, to the environment, to a particular community. That's very difficult. They have no financial incentive to keep that promise. There's a huge financial incentive to keep the promise to the customer. If Coca-Cola buys Odwalla, they're not going to put corn syrup in the formula because that destroys what Odwalla is.
>
> We've looked at a couple of natural meat companies, and it's pretty obvious to us that creating an all-natural, even organic, meat product is very difficult to do, it's very time intensive, and it's not well suited to factory farming. So the companies that are working in that natural, organic meat category tend to have a real commitment to family farms because those two things are very closely tied together. They can't actually get a natural, organic meat product unless they support these family farms and family farm practices.[13]

If building the company's values into the brand is the best strategy on the customer commitment side, building the company's values into the ownership structure is probably the best strategy on the community commitment side. Employee stock ownership programs (ESOPs) are particularly attractive to many mission-driven entrepreneurs because they ensure that the workers who helped build the business will have a strong say in how it operates going forward. Then, when values conflicts arise, the employees themselves will be the ones who have to make the tough decisions.

▪▪ Invent new instruments

Necessity is the mother of invention, so it is not surprising that the need for additional capital has given rise to some unusual new financing vehicles.

One of the most original structures I encountered was a debt-equity combination invented by Pura Vida Coffee, a Fair Trade coffee company with a focus on the institutional market, particularly colleges and universities. Pura Vida is the product of a friendship between two business school classmates, one who felt called to full-time ministry and service to the poor in Costa Rica, and one who pursued a successful career in high-tech but never forgot his dream of using business to have a social impact and mission.

▪ ▪

PURA VIDA COFFEE

Years in business:	8 (founded in 1998)
Start-up capital:	$1.5 million
Annual sales (2005):	$5 million projected for 2006
Corporate form:	Hybrid nonprofit/for-profit
Business:	Fair-trade coffee, cocoa, and tea

▪ ▪

John Sage, the high-tech mogul, and Chris Dearnley, the minister, started Pura Vida to purchase Fair Trade coffee from Costa Rican farmers and use the proceeds to fund social services in the farmers' home communities. Today their business has racked up significant accomplishments in its four areas of "desired impact": providing living wages for farmers by buying coffee at Fair Trade prices, educating consumers about the benefits of Fair Trade through sales on college campuses, using profits from the business to support at-risk children and families in its coffee-producing communities, and creating a viable business model as an example for others.[14]

The firm is so successful that it became the subject of a case study by its founders' alma mater, the Harvard Business School. At one point, a Harvard professor and sometime advisor challenged them by saying, "You talk a lot about the rigor and discipline in the marketplace and why you structured this as a for-profit and so on and so forth, but until you subject yourself to the rigor and discipline of the capital market and can attract other people's money, really all this is an expensive hobby."[15]

Accepting that challenge, Sage eventually created—and sold—a unique debt instrument with an equity-like sweetener at the end. He sold $2 million in $50,000 notes, carrying a low market interest rate, payable over five to eight years. The unique feature of these notes was that, once they were paid off, the investor would be entitled to give an equity-like claim on 1 percent of Pura Vida's future earnings to the charity of his or her choice. This provision was attractive to investors and to Pura Vida, which could still maintain the credibility of its status as being 100 percent owned by charity.[16]

Although this strategy was successful in the short term, it has created some long-term problems that Sage is now trying to address with a Series B offering.

> Now, the problem is when you finance with that much debt, you create real heavy liabilities for yourself. The principal and interest obligations are such that it's taking a lot of the working capital that we need to fund our growth now. It's made it very difficult to attract conventional financing. Some of the irony of all of this is that in many ways the fortunes of

the company have improved dramatically and there's much less risk. But we've really put ourselves in a box.

So we are in the process of taking out a Series B round. And we are going to go back to our Series A guys and encourage them to convert their A into straight B equity. If I can get, let's say, three-quarters of my Series A guys to agree, that will immediately lighten the debt level on the balance sheet dramatically. It will lower the principal and interest payment substantially. The money we save we can invest in growth opportunities right in front of us [that] will take the company to a much higher level much faster and accelerate the pace at which we can all get philanthropic leverage.[17]

By early January 2006, Sage had persuaded a majority of his Series A debt holders to "flip" into equity. In addition, he had launched a Series C equity round to bring in another $2 million to fund the company's ongoing growth.

An even more ambitious invention is Upstream 21, a holding company that is planning to acquire "small, locally owned, private companies with products or services and business practices that are designed to benefit and sustain their employees, their communities and the environment. . . . The Company's mission is to create a family of such businesses by acquiring them and operating them as wholly-owned subsidiaries."[18]

The brainchild of Leslie Christian and Bryan Redd, Upstream 21 is expressly designed as a vehicle for channeling capital to mission-driven businesses on mission-friendly terms. The idea was spawned as a solution to the legacy problem, providing owners of values-based businesses an opportunity to sell their businesses to a buyer that would preserve their values. It has evolved into a broader concept with the potential for solving a broader range of business issues. As Christian described it,

We're creating a liquidity event, not necessarily an exit strategy. It could be for any number of reasons—needing capital, transition for investors who want out, or founder exit.

But we're also creating this community of businesses that
have in common independent entrepreneurial spirit, environmental consciousness, social mission, and [a desire] to
thrive. They don't want to give up their independence, but
they don't want to be vulnerable either. So we buy them,
but we buy them with a built-in contract and commitment
to letting them continue. It's not about having a holding
company that's a big brother or parent . . . it's a federation.[19]

The rules of the "federation," spelled out in the Articles of
Incorporation, are unusual in two important respects. First, in
direct contrast to prevailing ideas about the primacy of maximizing shareholder value, these articles specifically *require* the
holding company to make decisions in the "best interests" of all
stakeholders. Specifically, the articles state that

the best interests of the Company shall include due consid-
eration of: the Company's and its subsidiaries' social, legal
and economic effects on their employees, customers and
suppliers and on the communities and geographic areas in
which the Company and its subsidiaries operate; the long-
term as well as short-term interests of the Company and its
shareholders; and the Company's and its subsidiaries'
effects on the environment.[20]

Second, the articles establish an unusual stock structure
designed to ensure appropriate voting representation for the
various stakeholder groups. The articles establish two classes of
stock: Class A and Class B. Class A shares come in three flavors:
Series 1, reserved for members of the board of directors; Series
2, reserved for individuals buying stock directly from the company; and Series 3, reserved for employees. The Class B shares
may be purchased by anyone, enabling them to be sold in the
secondary market, thereby providing an exit for close-in shareholders without giving up control. While all shares have voting
rights, on "Extraordinary Actions," shareholders vote by series,

and a two-thirds vote against the action by any two of the three close-in shareholders' groups can kill it.

This is a particularly elaborate attempt to balance the claims of multiple stakeholders. A simpler approach—the idea of having voting and nonvoting classes of stock—has been used successfully by family-owned firms and cooperatives seeking outside capital while retaining control. Accompanied by a stream of dividend payments, this option worked well for at least two of the co-ops I interviewed, Equal Exchange and Organic Valley Family of Farms.

▨▨ Exit with care

"What's your exit strategy?" is a question that became infamous during the dot-com bubble of the late 1990s. In that particular gilded age, entrepreneurs focused their energies on building "designer companies" in which the company itself was the product offering and the goal was to exit the business by exchanging company ownership for cash—often before any true value had been established. By the end of the era, a lot of money had changed hands, but very little new value had actually been created.

Given that all-too-recent history, it's not surprising that the *e*-word has acquired something of a bad reputation. In the post-bubble debates over the question of "Built to flip—or built to last?" as *Fast Company* magazine once framed it,[21] most mission-driven entrepreneurs land squarely in the "built to last" category.

Ironically, this makes the question of exit even more important. The critical question for mission-driven entrepreneurs, as noted above, is this: how do you ensure that the mission-based, nonfinancial values of your business survive beyond your own involvement and the involvement of your idealistic early investors? This is the legacy problem, and it is precisely the problem that the sale of Ben & Jerry's failed to address.

The key to achieving a more satisfactory outcome is to address the issue from the outset—or at least from the very first time the firm takes in outside investment, or Other People's

Money (OPM), as it is sometimes called. The basic problem is that outside investors—and, indeed, founders themselves—need liquidity, especially when they are ready to cash out at the end. In financially driven businesses with outside investors, the exit is typically accomplished by selling the business to another company (acquisition) or to the public (through an initial public offering, or IPO). In the case of single-bottom-line businesses, either of these outcomes is considered a win as long as the price is right. In the case of a mission-driven firm, the story is not so simple. There are at least three common problems at exit:

- It is difficult to ensure that the founding values of the firm will be preserved when the ownership changes. If the company ends up being publicly traded, it's almost (but not quite!) impossible.
- The interests of founder-owner(s) and the outside investors who have bankrolled the business may diverge. It is not uncommon for investors to want to realize a return on their investment through a sale of the company before the founding entrepreneur is ready to let go.
- Finally, many mission-driven businesses do not have the kind of growth potential that would make them attractive acquisition or IPO candidates. They may be solvent, profitable, and growing but still unlikely to generate the kind of explosive growth that many investors like to buy into.

Failure to address the exit problem casts a very long shadow over the whole mission-driven sector. It makes it difficult for investors to take a position in the early stages of these companies because they don't know whether, how, or when they will get their money out. It makes it difficult for entrepreneurs to raise money or to ensure that the values they have built into the business will survive their departure.

Dal LaMagna, the founder of Tweezerman, introduced in Chapter 2, built his exit as carefully as he built his company. As he explained,

When it came time for me to sell it, I intentionally tried to close it without having to sacrifice the values that I had built into it. And so I handled the sale of the company myself.

I had four rules: one, that no employee would be laid off as a consequence of the sale—except myself, of course. Two, [that] the business would not be moved from where it was. I wasn't interested in anyone buying the business and moving it to another place and driving everyone crazy. Third, the company would continue to practice responsible capitalism as defined by our best practices. And fourth, whoever bought the company would pay a lot of money.

But that was not only for me, because I had gotten to the point where I had accomplished one goal, which was that every one of my employees would be a shareholder in the company. So at the end, I had 192 shareholders. Ten percent of the company was held by 12 or 13 people, and another 10 percent was held by everybody else in the ESOP. The thing I was most proud of is that I was able to accomplish that goal.[22]

In the end, the purchaser, Zwilling J. A. Henckels, a privately held German firm founded in 1731, agreed to all four conditions—plus a payout on the ESOP, which matured with the sale. All told, Henckels agreed to pay the Tweezerman employees a "stay-on bonus," which amounted to about $800,000, and La-Magna himself distributed $1 million as "gifts" to his 200 U.S. and 135 Indian employees. And LaMagna's practices of "responsible capitalism"—including the practice of giving away 5 percent of profits each year—continue.

■■LESSONS LEARNED

The most important lesson to take away from this chapter is the one expressed in the title: for mission-driven entrepreneurs, it is critical to finance your *independence*—not just your business. All of the strategies suggested in this chapter and elsewhere in this book—from bootstrapping to organic growth to seeking values-based investors to using debt rather than equity—are designed to minimize the control that outside investors can exert.

This is not to say that investors are evil or inherently hostile to mission-driven businesses. It is simply to recognize that there is a market for investments, just as there is a market for products. While some investors shop for "social returns," the vast majority shop for financial returns, which they evaluate in terms of risk, reward, and liquidity—the ability to get their money out of the business.

The needs of investors are a large part of the aforementioned legacy problem. This is a very real issue, but I worry about its framing as an endgame issue. It must be considered from the very first time the business seeks outside capital. My advice is simple: when it comes to taking in Other People's Money, begin with the end in mind—that is, have a clear strategy for satisfying their need for an exit that doesn't jeopardize the mission of the business.■ ■

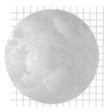

CHAPTER FIVE

Build Your Values into the Brand

DESPITE THE DIVERSITY of the businesses I interviewed, the vast majority shared one important competitive strategy: differentiation. A handful were engaged in head-to-head competition on price, but most had managed to carve out unique market positions with superior margins that could be used to cover the "extra" costs of their environmental and social commitments.

In some cases, such as the entire organic-foods sector, the interests of producers and consumers are directly aligned. It usually costs more to grow food organically, but consumers are willing to pay extra because they understand and value what they are getting. In other cases, such as New Belgium Brewing Company, consumers are willing to pay a premium price for a high-quality product, defined by the taste of the beer—not by all the superior attributes of the company that made it. But the premium price generates higher margins, which the owners can then *choose* to spend on activities that yield social and environmental benefits.

As mission-driven entrepreneurs attempt to build their values into the brand, it is important to understand what customers truly value and are willing to pay for. As Jacquelyn Ottman, the leading authority on "green marketing," has written,

> Although a small number of highly committed consumers will sacrifice in the name of altruism, the great majority of consumers, understandably, are still not prepared to give up such coveted product attributes as performance, quality, convenience, or price. Product efficacy continues to

strongly influence consumer purchase decisions. As too many green marketers learned the hard way, environmentally preferable products still need to work, and they still must be priced competitively or project superior primary benefits in order to attract a wide market.

Historical reluctance to pay a premium for green goods seems to be softening, as consumers connect environmental responsibility with health or other direct benefits. Sales of organically grown "clean" foods, natural cosmetics, and cottons grown without pesticides demonstrate that when it comes to green products, the greater the self interest, the greater the perceived threat, the greater the willingness to pay.[1]

Country Natural Beef

Country Natural Beef (formerly Oregon Country Beef) is a great example of both the power of differentiation in a commodity business, and the importance of aligning the values of producer and consumer. Doc and Connie Hatfield started Oregon Country Beef, a rancher-owned cooperative, in 1987 because beef prices got so low they were going out of business. The breakthrough came when Connie walked into a fitness center in Bend, Oregon, and asked what people there thought about red meat. As she tells the story,

> This 25-year-old "Jack LaLanne," with big muscles, almost skipped out, and said, "I recommend it at least three times a week. But we're having the hardest time getting Argentina beef in here to Bend, Oregon." "Argentina beef, why is that?" "Well, it's produced without hormones, without antibiotics, and it's short- fed, it doesn't have all that fat in it."
>
> I drove home, and I said to myself: You call yourself a rancher. You live 55 miles from where this man is, who says they need meat from Argentina that doesn't have hormones and antibiotics, and that's exactly what we're raising. Right here. We're raising it; we've just never marketed it.[2]

Armed with that insight, the Hatfields invited 14 ranching families to a meeting in their living room and formed the nucleus of Oregon Country Beef, which is described on its Web site as "a cooperative linking ranchers and consumers for the benefit of both."[3] Eighteen years later, when I interviewed the Hatfields, the co-op had grown to 55 member and prospective member families representing 106,000 cows grazing on 4 million acres of land—and doing about $40 million a year in business.[4]

■ ■

COUNTRY NATURAL BEEF

Years in business:	19 (founded in 1987)
Start-up capital:	NA
Annual sales (2005):	$40 million
Corporate form:	Cooperative
Business:	Natural beef

■ ■

The co-op itself has no employees and virtually no assets. Doc said, "Aside from our accounts receivable, which are only two weeks old at the oldest, if we took all our other assets in this $40 million business, [we'd] end up with less than $5,000 and maybe one computer and some ear tags and labels."[5]

What it does have, however, is a very strong brand. Marketers tend to think of brands in terms of the four Ps: product, price, place, and promotion. Country Natural Beef is highly differentiated in all four dimensions, as summarized below.

Product

The core product is differentiated as "natural," which in this case means raised from birth without hormones, steroids, antibiotics, or feed additives; grazed on 4 million acres of open range managed under the co-op's own rigorous "Grazewell Principles"; finished on a vegetarian diet in a specialty feedlot; and humanely slaughtered by a meat processor who shares the values of the producer co-op. The result is a lean beef that grades out as High

Select/Low Choice (rather than the more common—and widely touted—USDA Choice or Prime). The co-op is adamant on the virtues of its grading, saying, "We do not feed our cattle to grade out at a High Choice or Prime Grade as it is ecologically indefensible to feed excessive amounts of grain to fatten up an animal past the point of health—both for the animal and the consumer. Our beef is quality lean beef that not only tastes good but is good for you."[6] It is "natural" rather than "organic" because it would be impossible to meet the organic standard of "100 percent organically certified feed" in cattle raised on the open range.

Price

Despite those last two caveats, Country Natural Beef commands a small price premium in the marketplace. It is not clear whether it's the health, flavor, or environmental-stewardship benefits that the consumer is paying for, but the combination definitely characterizes the brand and commands a premium price.

Place

Country Natural Beef is as picky about its customers as it is about its producers. Its sales have grown dramatically over the last 10 years—nearly doubling in volume in 2005 alone. The beef is sold through about 22 premium quality restaurants, which call out the brand on their menus, and about two dozen supermarkets and small chains. Whole Foods, the co-op's largest account, has taken the brand as far east as Kansas and Louisiana, and has encouraged the Oregon group to work with local ranchers in Texas and New Mexico to replicate the model in the Southwest. Rather than pursue, or even accept, new retail accounts, Country Natural Beef has grown as its core accounts have grown and has declined to supply competing retailers whose values were not congruent with its own. As Connie put it, "They sell commodity beef. We sell de-commodified beef."[7]

Promotion

While brand building typically requires oversize marketing budgets, Country Natural Beef spends very little on marketing.

Instead, it has built its business on relationships: Relationships among the rancher-producers, who have built a strong community of shared values and who maintain their connection through weekly conference calls and semiannual meetings conducted in a circle and operated by consensus. Relationships with customers, who are honored through an annual Customer Appreciation Day that brings together ranchers, meat cutters, restaurateurs, and supermarket owners from around the Pacific Northwest for an old-fashioned family picnic at one of the member ranches. And finally, relationships with consumers who meet the ranchers face-to-face in the supermarkets where Country Natural Beef is sold. According to Doc,

> The in-store idea was that we had no money to provide promotion. Most retailers want some kind of promotion, and a real rancher in the store is a huge benefit to them.
>
> As soon as we did it, we realized that it totally changed the view of the rancher. People are different once they interact with a customer. You can talk about these things forever, but once somebody spends two days in a store talking to consumers, they realize that people who want to buy a known product of some perceived health benefit are rational, reasonable, well-intentioned folks. It makes that tie between the ranch and the consumer real, and not just something you talk about.[8]

Eileen Fisher Inc.

At Eileen Fisher, the women's clothing company, the four Ps are purpose, product, practice, and profitability—a mission statement rather than a marketing strategy.[9] The company's purpose—"To inspire simplicity, creativity and delight through connection and great design"—is thoroughly realized in its products and retail stores. Simplicity, timeless designs, fine fabrics and yarns, and an understanding of the lives and preferences of its target market of women aged 35–50 provide the basis for the company's product differentiation—and timeless value. The company's public persona is primarily about the clothes and how they meet the needs of the busy women who wear them.

■ ■

EILEEN FISHER INC.

Years in business:	22 (founded in 1984)
Start-up capital:	$350
Annual sales (2005):	$194 million
Corporate form:	Private for-profit
Business:	Women's fashion apparel

■ ■

But there's another Eileen Fisher story—the story of a company that pays as much attention to its practices as to its profits, beginning with its manufacturing practices. Fifteen percent of the company's clothes are manufactured in the United States at U.S. wages, while the balance are produced in China under a rigorous set of standards known as Social Accountability 8000 (SA 8000), which cover health and safety, wages, working hours, and minimum working ages. Eileen Fisher is one of a handful of U.S. companies that apply this standard to their manufacturing facilities.

The company strives "to create an environment that inspires our best work, individually and in connection." In addition to a generous profit-sharing program, employees get an annual $1,000 education benefit and $1,000 wellness benefit, which can be spent on massages, nutritional consultations, reflexology, spa visits, and gym equipment. There are free on-site classes in yoga, tai chi, dance movement, and stress reduction. After 10 years on the job, workers receive a $5,000 bonus and an extra week's vacation, to be used on a trip. Not to mention the clothing discount on Eileen Fisher fashions . . .[10]

Finally, the company's practices support the community. Eileen Fisher has consistently donated a percentage of its pretax profits to charitable organizations that support women's health and well-being and women's independence and empowerment.

In this case, differentiation creates profits, and profits create opportunities to confer benefits. And because Eileen Fisher remains privately held, the benefits strongly reflect the values of the founder.

Give Something Back Business Products

This California office-products vendor represents a third differentiation strategy, which the founders have christened the "Newman's Own" business strategy.[11] According to cofounder Mike Hannigan,

> We've been in business since 1991 and, despite the implications of the name, Give Something Back, we are a competitive business in the office supply space. Our competitors include Office Depot and Staples. We sell business-to-business office supplies, furniture and printing, and we do it in a way to [maximize] profit. The difference, and that's where the name comes from, is that when we earn a profit, instead of having the profit go to stockholders, our profits are donated to the communities that we sell to in support of their nonprofit organizations. And we ask our customers and our employees to decide which organizations [to support].
>
> [That approach] has been very successful . . . as an additional motivation for our customers to use us. We've grown phenomenally over the last 13 years. We're the biggest independent in California now. We're not as big as the national superstores, but our goal ultimately is to aim in that direction. And, the success is not based on any kind of sacrifice. Our customers don't make any sacrifices. We're not making sacrifices. I make a very comfortable living. Every employee here makes what they would make at another company. We compete for labor. Our customers are very satisfied. The people who work here are very satisfied. And the

other beneficiary is that the profits, instead of being sucked
out of the community, are put back into the community to
build the capacity of the community and to enrich the quality of life in this community.[12]

. . . .

GIVE SOMETHING BACK BUSINESS PRODUCTS

Years in business:	15 (founded in 1991)
Start-up capital:	$40,000
Annual sales (2005):	$24 million
Corporate form:	Private for-profit
Business:	Office supplies

. . . .

Hannigan and his partner, Sean Marx, started their business
in 1991 with $40,000 of their own money. By 2004, they were giv-
ing away roughly $500,000 a year in profits. The key to their suc-
cess is to be businesspeople first, philanthropists second.

[I]n terms of the sensibility or the motivation that I bring to
it, I think that's [something] that is in most people. Given
the opportunity to make a good living, a comparable living
that you're making now in a way that you can, at the end of
the day, say, "Not only did I benefit and my family benefit,
but I did something good for the community and a lot of
people benefited." I don't see a whole lot of people who
wouldn't jump at that opportunity.
    So I see myself as less different than most other people
except that I've found this vehicle to be able to do both,
and it's turned out to be very successful here because the
core principle from the beginning was serving the interests
of the community. But we also had this firm understanding
that in order to achieve a success as a business we need to
be business people, listen to our customers like business
people, and treat our employees like business people.[13]

■■LESSONS LEARNED

Each of these companies used differentiation differently:

- Country Natural Beef "de-commodified" its beef by building a unique, fully integrated production system that created a unique product: lean, healthy, drug-free beef—a powerful cluster of consumer health benefits. It charged a premium for its products and returned that money to its rancher-owners so that they could continue their lifestyle and environmental stewardship.
- Give Something Back Business Products "de-commodified" the office-supply business by matching its competitors on price and service, while beating them on the distribution of profits. Customers got the feel-good benefit of contributing to the community without having to pay more for the privilege.
- Eileen Fisher competed on product quality and design in an industry that is all about differentiation. It then chose to share a portion of its profits with its employees and customer community.

In the case of Country Natural Beef and Give Something Back Business Products, the values of the business are built into the value of the brand—that is, they are an explicit part of what customers are paying for. At Country Natural Beef, those values command a price premium. At Give Something Back, they create customer loyalty.

At Eileen Fisher, the relationship between values and brand is much subtler. It is clear that the firm's customers are willing to pay a premium price for the company's elegant designs and luxurious fabrics—and it is clear that Eileen Fisher and the staff that she has assembled are deeply committed to the many practices that embody their values. It may also be true that the culture they've created helps to attract and retain talent in an industry where talent is paramount. But the cultural values of the firm, while clearly a point of pride, are not necessarily built into the brand—and may be more vulnerable as a result.

The relationship between differentiation and scale is less clear. Differentiation strategies are sometimes referred to as "niche" strategies—strategies aimed at smaller, more focused target markets, in contrast to "mass market" strategies. Thus, almost by definition, they are not built to scale as well as mass-market or commodity strategies explicitly designed to take advantage of traditional economies of scale. If the entire cost structure of the business is built around a premium price point, simple increases in volume will not necessarily lead to economies of scale. A deeper understanding of the relationship between cost, volume, and profit is required to make a wholesale migration from niche to mass market.

But scale is relative. It may well be possible for mission-driven entrepreneurs to create the impact they are looking for without becoming mass-market competitors. And niches come in all sizes: they need not be small.

On the other hand, there is nothing that says a mission-driven business with a differentiated strategy cannot succeed against mass-market competitors. The Newman's Own/Give Something Back model bears watching. As Mike Hannigan put it:

Many people ask, "How can you run a successful business and give your profits away?" Well, you know, every successful business gives its profits away. . . . It either goes as dividends or it's to be invested in the company, and eventually it goes out as dividends to the shareholders. Every company gives its profits away, so we don't do anything different. We just give to a different place.[14]

CHAPTER SIX

Match Manufacturing to Mission

DAVID GREEN is a miracle worker.

The founder of a nonprofit called Project Impact, he helps restore sight to the blind—not one person at a time, but thousands of people at a time. He is a social entrepreneur in the Ashoka[1] sense of the word:

> The . . . social entrepreneur . . . finds what is not working and solves the problem by changing the system, spreading the solution and persuading entire societies to take new leaps. . . .
>
> Identifying and solving large-scale social problems requires a social entrepreneur because only the entrepreneur has the committed vision and inexhaustible determination to persist until they have transformed an entire system.[2]

In the case of David Green, who was recognized as an Ashoka Fellow in 2002 and as a MacArthur "genius" award recipient in 2004, the initial problem was blindness in India. There, as in most of the developing world, roughly 5 to 6 percent of the populace over 65 and nearly 1 percent of the population as a whole was blind due to cataracts—*operable* cataracts.

The technology to solve that problem has existed for a long time. It's a relatively quick and simple surgical implant of a manufactured intraocular lens (IOL). In the United States, the surgery takes about an hour and can cost several thousand dollars, a price that would be prohibitive for most people in India and in most of the developing world. Fortunately, thanks to the efforts of Green and his colleagues, many cataract victims can take advantage of that surgery either at no cost or for a fraction of that price *without* government subsidies.

Green's basic approach is to take a low-volume, high-margin business and turn it into a high-volume, low-margin business— a strategy that is beginning to come into favor with multinationals as they begin to develop their own "bottom of the pyramid" strategies.[3] However, where their goal is profit, his goal is service.

Green calls his system "compassionate capitalism," and it has several distinctive features, the first of which is pricing. In the Aravind Eye Hospital, in Madurai, India, where Green got his start as a social entrepreneur, and in the hundred or so institutions around the world to which he has exported his ideas, the pricing system is multitiered. About a third of the patients are treated for free; a third pay about 65 percent of the cost; and the remaining third pay a price that is high enough to cover the organization's operating costs *and* generate a profit that can be used for growth.

The key to achieving "profitability" with that kind of pricing is to keep costs low. And the keys to that are volume and control. In the programs that Green sets up, a surgeon will typically do 20 operations in a morning with a highly efficient team approach. In China, by contrast, the average surgeon will do something like 14 cataract operations per *year*. The surgery itself is simple and repetitive, so performing it as a batch operation dramatically reduces costs.[4] At Aravind, this approach has enabled the organization to scale from an 11-bed hospital in 1978 to a facility performing 5,000 cataract operations per year in 1983, when Green arrived in India, to a four-hospital chain performing 200,000 cataract surgeries per year today.[5]

But that's only half the story. The other half is on the materials side in a company called Aurolab, which Green helped found in 1992 when Aravind's supply of donated intraocular lenses

(IOLs) began to dry up, due to changes in U.S. regulations. Despite knowing little about business and even less about manufacturing, he decided that he would figure out how to manufacture affordable lenses himself. The operation he founded now manufactures 600,000–700,000 IOLs annually, roughly 10 percent of the world market. A quarter of its output goes to Aravind's four eye hospitals, with the balance exported to 86 countries around the globe. Between 1992 and 2005, the average price of IOLs made by other companies dropped from $300–$400 to about $100–$150, while Aurolab's average cost of manufacturing dropped from $10 to about $4–$5 apiece.[6]

Green described his approach in an interview for the Ashoka Changemakers Web site:

> Basically, we use the same equipment and manufacturing process and we fulfill the same regulatory requirements for quality as other companies do, whether they are in America or Europe or elsewhere. But Aurolab sells the lenses for less, not only because their costs are lower but because they chose to price them lower—because our goal is maximizing service rather than maximizing profit. . . .
>
> [I]t really doesn't cost that much to make something. [I begin by] demystifying the cost and the technology by walking around the industry and checking things out—by seeing manufacturing and doing some estimates of how much it really costs them to make stuff based on their equipment and how old it is, whether they've amortized it, their labor costs and cost of the raw material.
>
> I make the cost structure transparent so that at least I can see if something can be made affordable. We do everything we can to sculpt each cost and each margin along the way—for any given supply chain—to fit our ultimate target price that ensures affordability for the end user.
>
> Then I see whether I can work with ethical people to deliver a product that's going to meet quality standards and still be affordable—whether we can produce it with a start-

up and operating cost that creates a price that is affordable
to our target populations, which are basically poor to mid-
dle-class people in developing countries. My goal isn't to
maximize return on investment to shareholders, but to
maximize number of people served. It's a humanitarian
goal.[7]

To date, Green has applied his model of "compassionate capitalism" to cataract surgery, intraocular lenses, surgical sutures,
and hearing aids. But he believes that in the developing world it
has applications in areas as diverse as AIDS treatment, comput-
ers, solar energy, and social and financial services. And his hope
is that others will embrace his model and actually compete with
him in the areas he enters. He takes the risk, he develops the
model, he proves that it works profitably—and then if the big
for-profit firms come into his territory to compete on his terms,
he's happy.

I have no interest in being a producer or seller of hearing
aids. What I do care about is creating a paradigm shift in
how people view how they can make a product and service
affordable and available to a greater number of the human
family.[8]

American Apparel Inc.

In a completely different industry and setting, American Apparel
has pulled off a different kind of miracle: a U.S.-based manufacturing operation that pays its garment workers an average
wage of $12.59 an hour and competes successfully against off-
shore producers, who pay as little as 9 cents an hour.[9]
This performance, which has catapulted American Apparel into
the position of being the largest garment factory in the United
States, runs counter to all the prevailing wisdom in this industry—
and in a host of other industries in which most people believe the
United States can no longer compete. Fully 96 percent of all cloth-

ing in the United States is imported because "everyone knows" that you can't afford to make clothes here anymore.[10]

. . . .

AMERICAN APPAREL INC.

Years in business:	9 (founded in 1997)
Start-up capital:	NA
Annual sales (2005):	$250 million (estimated)
Corporate form:	Private for-profit
Business:	T-shirts and youth fashion apparel

. . . .

Everyone, that is, except Dov Charney and Marty Bailey. Charney is the name synonymous with American Apparel—the company's "founder, owner, visionary, and passion," while Bailey, VP of operations, is the back-shop guy who helps "facilitate his vision and passion as effectively and efficiently as possible."[11] Bailey, a 21-year veteran of the garment business, is the one who experienced firsthand the export of garment-industry jobs from the U.S. South and the import of manufacturing problems from offshore producers.

At one point, he was working for a small company in Tennessee that had moved all of its manufacturing offshore and had asked him to go to Miami, where its freight forwarder was located, to assess the cost structure of the company's business. After three weeks,

> [W]hen the owner came in and asked me what I thought, I told him I thought he should close Florida; he should pull everything back into Tennessee. He [said], "Well, why?" And I said, "How much money are you saving on labor by sewing in the Dominican Republic or Haiti?" "We're saving about $2.40 a dozen." I said, "Gary, it's costing you $6.24 a dozen to get it there and back." They didn't have enough volume to fill the containers and everything was rushed, and at the end of the day, they were rushing themselves out of business.[12]

It was the same story on a much larger scale at Fruit of the Loom, where Bailey worked for 15 years. After spending his first 10 years opening new manufacturing facilities in the U.S. Southeast, he spent the next 5 years shutting down those plants and moving production offshore. Through that experience, he says, "I had an opportunity there to see the bad side of offshore manufacturing. I don't mean bad as in evil; I mean bad as in hidden costs and things that your labor dollars cannot compensate for." These hidden costs included rush charges, quality-control problems, missed market windows, and excessive freight charges based on partial container loads. Eventually he came to the conclusion that "if somebody had the right business model, they could be very successful [as a domestic manufacturer]—in some cases, just cleaning up what everybody else has screwed up. In Dov's case, his beliefs fit with what I believe in, and this was my opportunity to prove it."[13]

Bailey believes there are four key elements to the success of American Apparel's manufacturing operation, all of them made possible by the firm's decision to remain in the United States.

Quality

"If you're going to try to do this and you're going to offer the same stuff that everybody else offers, whether it's from China or Central America or anywhere else, you're just kidding yourself."[14] American Apparel charges a premium for its products and distinguishes itself in terms of the quality of the yarns it uses; the tightness of its weaves; its on-site, real-time control over defects in workmanship; and the tight links between design and manufacturing, which enable it to respond quickly to fashion trends.

Market focus

"Our workforce consists of our targeted market, so we have ready-made focus groups every day."[15] From the factory to the Web site to the retail stores to the customers on the street, American Apparel appears to operate to the beat of its target market of "trend-conscious young adults."[16] There is no delay between idea and execution. "We can approve a design, and literally, if I approved a design this morning, we should have a shippable product in our warehouse this afternoon."[17]

Quick turns

Market responsiveness is only one of the benefits of quick turns on inventory. Of equal benefit is the ability to free up cash from work-in-process inventory and use it for other purposes. Bailey's response to the inventory problem was to move from a loose assembly line to a tight manufacturing team approach. When he set up a pilot team of 11 people to demonstrate what he had in mind, he invited Charney's investment partner, Sam Lim, to take a look. "I remember Sam coming out, we looked at it for about three minutes, and I asked him what he thought, and he said, 'When can you change the rest of it?'"[18] Five months later, the entire plant—65 teams—was switched over, tripling output from 30,000 to 90,000 pieces a day, while increasing staff by only 20 percent.

Customer service

With production in-house in the United States, American Apparel is able to be extremely responsive to its customers without maintaining the huge stocks of finished-goods inventory required by a firm that manufactures offshore and makes shipments by the container. "Seventy-five-plus percent of our business is for piece orders. It might be six of these, and three of those, and eight of them. And at the end of the day, you've got a nice little order, but you have to make sure you can put your hands on individual pieces. If, for some reason, I don't have that piece of stock, I can tell the customer specifically when I will and follow through. I think when you're making a viable commitment to your customers, you've got a leg up because people are tired of hearing 'Yeah, yeah, yeah,' and then get frustrated because it's actually 'No, no, no.'"[19]

By keeping its manufacturing in the United States—and in fact housing its entire 3,000-plus core workforce in a single eight-story building in downtown Los Angeles—American Apparel is definitely running counter to the prevailing wisdom of the field. But its employment policies and benefits are what have really attracted media attention. In the industry that spawned the labor movement and invented the concept of sweatshops, American Apparel offers its workers the highest wages in the industry; year-round employment and job security; affordable health-care and dental insurance for workers and their families; and a host of unusual benefits, including company-subsidized lunches, bus passes, free ESL classes, on-site masseurs, assistance in enrolling in the federal Earned Income Credit program, and free and low-cost access to a host of financial services.[20]

It's no surprise that the company's workforce is highly stable, happy, and productive—a huge asset to the business. What is less clear is the causal relationship between the profitable, vertically integrated business model and the generous employee-benefits package. Is it worker productivity that makes it possible for American Apparel to compete with companies that pay their employees less than a dollar a day? Or is it the cleverness and efficiency of the overall operation that makes it possible to offer employees such a generous package of pay and benefits?

For now, the two are intertwined. As the company's Web site puts it, "Ultimately, it is vertical integration, an efficient system that cuts out the middlemen, that enables the company to be sweatshop free. Because we do not outsource to local or developing-nation sweatshops, the entire process is time-efficient and the company can respond at breakneck speed to demand. This enables us to be competitive within the global market."[21]

GreenDisk

David Beschen's company, GreenDisk, lies at the other end of the manufacturing spectrum: he outsources *everything*.

. . . .

GREENDISK

Years in business:	14 (founded in 1992)
Start-up capital:	$150,000
Annual sales (2005):	$2 million+
Corporate form:	C corporation
Business:	Audited electronic-waste recycling and recycled product manufacturing

. . . .

That was not always so. At one point, he managed four factories and a staff of 200, collecting obsolete product from major software vendors and recycling the paper manuals and diskettes. He also provided an audit trail to vendors, ensuring that their intellectual property had been destroyed and would not find its way onto the black market. It was a great business, growing 200–300 percent a year, until it ran into its own version of the perfect storm, in 1997.

We saw three things happen in one year. In one three- or four-month period, we saw the paper prices fall from $350 a ton to about $35 a ton, a 90 percent decline in the staple that had been paying our underlying costs.

Then the price of diskettes started to fall because of overproduction. The Chinese . . . doubled the world capacity for diskettes . . . so that drove the price of diskettes down. Another 90 percent loss in revenue. First the paper, then the diskettes.

Then the CD really took over. The transition from the 5¼-inch disk to the 3½-inch disk took over 10 years. The transition from the 3½-inch disk to the CD took about 10 minutes. No one foresaw that quick of a transition. And without exception, every company we dealt with went out of business, shut down, went bankrupt, merged with another company, was broken up and split up to become another company. No survivors. With one exception. Us.

We almost died. But we fought back. We transitioned very heavily. We got out of the service business. We began to outsource absolutely everything to a small network of nonprofit workshops. So we had a very flexible workforce with great scalability, and we didn't have to pay anybody anything when they weren't working. We got out of the labor-intensive part of the business, the actual software destruction, and just focused on that massive inventory we had built up of diskettes.[22]

Beschen's company has transitioned several times since then—his latest focus is on recycling a broader range of "technotrash" for a broader range of clients—but he's never been tempted to rebuild his manufacturing capacity. Instead, he has increased his cleverness at recycling other people's production and distribution capacity. He buys manufacturing "down time" (excess capacity) and transportation "back hauls" (returning trucks that would otherwise be empty). He buys his labor from sheltered workshops, providing them with valued contracts while eliminating the need to maintain a labor force of his own.

At the end of the day, he's a broker and a marketing guy. Although his business involves manufacturing, his mission does not require that he do it himself. This is in contrast to David Green's business, which required control over manufacturing to achieve a particular price point, and Marty Bailey's business, which required control over manufacturing in order to be sweatshop free and highly responsive to the youth fashion market. And although David Beschen sells recycled products as one aspect of his operation, his real business is a service: the audited and environmentally sensitive disposal of electronic waste. Outsourcing works just fine.

New Leaf Paper

Jeff Mendelsohn, of New Leaf Paper, is another manufacturer/distributor who doesn't do his own manufacturing—and he *is* in a product business. Even more unusual, he has big ideas about moving the entire paper industry in a more sustainable direction, beginning by leveraging his unique, factory-free papermaking strategy.

▪ ▪

NEW LEAF PAPER

Years in business:	8 (founded in 1998)
Start-up capital:	$10,000
Annual sales (2005):	$18.5 million
Corporate form:	Private for-profit (LLC)
Business:	Environmentally responsible paper production

▪ ▪

Mendelsohn is basically a brand builder. The mission of New Leaf Paper is "to be the leading national source for environmentally responsible, economically sound paper" and "to inspire—through our success—a fundamental shift toward environmental responsibility in the paper industry."[23] A key to success at present is an unusual product-development strategy that marries Mendelsohn's knowledge of paper producers with his knowledge of paper consumers to match the demand for environmentally responsible papers by using the excess capacity of existing paper mills.

Part of what we needed in order to have a mission of creating a sustainable paper industry was to have a vision of what that industry would look like. So we look for mills that embody those principles. And usually that means they have a competitive edge in making a better environmental paper. We go to their engineers and design products and manufacture them and market them.

Sometimes I wish I owned my own machines so I could control everything, but then I hear how difficult it is to make money in manufacturing these days, and certainly the risks are enormous when you own a machine and a facility because your fixed overhead is so high. So in some ways we're in a pretty enviable position in that we're able to create product lines and develop our own brands, but not have the associated risk of owning all the manufacturing.

And, frankly, we don't necessarily want our own manufacturing until there's a new paradigm of manufacturing out there. I am holding out, hoping that at some point there will be a smaller-scale design of a mill that embodies the principles of sustainability and is competitive. But for now, there are a lot of mills that have excess capacity, and their business models require them to be running constantly in order to cover all the fixed costs. So we're an attractive proposition to a lot of mills, because we can bring tons [of paper orders] without them needing to invest in marketing and branding.[24]

New Leaf Paper provides an interesting example of some of the inherent tensions at the intersection of mission, manufacturing, and scale. The company's ambitious mission is to move its entire industry in a more sustainable direction. For now, given the required scale economies of that industry, the goal is best achieved by aggregating demand and partnering with the most environmentally sustainable existing producers. And in an industry like paper, with extraordinarily high fixed costs, those relatively small orders can make the difference between profit and loss for New Leaf's manufacturing partners.

■■LESSONS LEARNED

Clearly, one of the major lessons learned in this area is that there is no one right way to approach manufacturing. There is a continuum from complete outsourcing to total integration, and any point along that line is at least theoretically possible. The question is, how is one to choose?

In a financially driven firm, the answer is to choose the point that maximizes profit, recognizing that this point will vary from industry to industry and company to company. In theory, it can be calculated fairly precisely based on plant capacity, inventory carrying costs, and shipping costs for raw materials and finished goods. In practice, things are a little more complicated than that, but the basic idea is the same: locate manufacturing capacity close to either raw materials or final markets, and bring it on line in the smallest increments you can get away with, given your market forecast and expected economies of scale.

All those considerations come into play in a mission-driven firm as well, but there are a couple of additional wrinkles. In a mission-driven firm, the first question to address is the relationship between mission and manufacturing.

If the *mission* requires manufacturing—a determination that is not always easy to make (per the example of New Leaf Paper)—then you need to do manufacturing, and the challenge is to figure out how to build manufacturing capacity slowly, cheaply, or in modular units. You don't want to jeopardize the mission by creating excess capacity, excess costs, or excessive requirements for outside capital. And you don't want to jeopardize sales by being forced to charge higher prices just because you have higher costs. (You may *choose* to charge a higher price based on your positioning, but as far as possible this should be a marketing choice, not a manufacturing requirement.)

If the mission does *not* require you to own your own manufacturing facilities, outsourcing may offer significant advantages without jeopardizing your social and/or environmental commitments. You simply need to make sure that those commitments are reflected in your outsourcing requirements. If you can't find (or create) vendors that can meet your standards, then perhaps your mission *does* require you to do manufacturing—and you just hadn't realized it! In that case, you want to be sure the business side of the equation will support your environmental and social goals at a scale on which you can afford to build and operate.

One of the keys to that may be to significantly reconceptualize the business, as each of these entrepreneurs did in his own industry:

Project Impact—Turned a low-volume, high-margin business into a high-volume, low-margin business.

American Apparel—Recognized the hidden costs of offshore production and the hidden benefits of vertical integration to create a cost-competitive, rapid-response domestic manufacturing operation.

GreenDisk—Divested itself of staff and facilities to reduce costs and gain flexibility in responding to rapidly changing market conditions.

New Leaf Paper—Aggregated demand to place orders with more environmentally sustainable facilities, thereby helping to tip the paper industry toward sustainability.

In all four cases, the commitment to mission came first, the need to limit capital investment came second, and a healthy dose of creativity—sparked by each company's mission commitment—came third. ■ ■

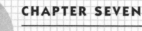

CHAPTER SEVEN

Morph Early and Often

GIFFORD PINCHOT III, author of the business classic *Intrapreneuring* and my mentor on entrepreneurship, has a dictum he's long sought to impress upon me: "Faster learning beats better planning." Waving this banner, he has encouraged hundreds of would-be entrepreneurs to jump into the game, make mistakes, stay light on their feet, learn from their mistakes, try again, make more mistakes, shift again—and, over time, blunder their way to success.

It's not that he's opposed to planning (although sometimes I wonder!); it's that he has a different idea of its purpose and role in achieving success. He challenges his students to do multiple iterations of their business plans, "morphing" (short for *metamorphosing*) their thinking before they ever get to the starting gate. This puts them in the habit of staying flexible, which is arguably the greatest key to success.

His theory is certainly borne out by the experience of the entrepreneurs I interviewed. Among the examples we've encountered so far:

- Organic Valley Family of Farms started as a produce operation but found its real opportunity in dairy.
- Seventh Generation started as a mail-order retailer of eco-goods but ended up manufacturing paper and cleaning products, sold in mainstream supermarkets.
- GreenDisk started out in the floppy-disk-recycling business but ended up in the technotrash business as its market evolved.

The three organizations profiled below offer further insights into the morphing phenomenon.

ScriptSave

ScriptSave, which offers discounts on prescription drugs primarily to seniors, is an example of a continually morphing business, beginning with the morphing of its founder, a serial entrepreneur named Charlie Horn. He came to the pharmacy world from the insurance and benefits business, in which he had started two previous companies. The second company brought him into the world of "value added" insurance benefits, such as dental programs, vision benefits, and prescription drug plans. From there, he spotted the opportunity that became ScriptSave.

> I started the company by calling a lot of insurance companies that did not offer prescription drug coverage, particularly to senior citizens. It became evident that if they could provide their members with, not an insurance benefit, but a way to save money on prescription drugs, they would be thrilled. So my challenge was to find a way to put a program like that together and then find a way to earn money to support [it].[1]

He did that by recruiting a diverse coalition of corporate players in the pharmaceutical and insurance industries, wisely appealing to the self-interest of each, and parlaying their needs into both a profitable business and a significant source of benefits for seniors. By the end of 2005, 11 years after the company's founding, ScriptSave had saved its customers a verified total of $1 billion.

His coalition includes the following:

- Organizational sponsors (such as insurance companies, employers, and associations), who offer the ScriptSave card to their constituents as part of a benefits plan.

- Retail pharmacies that offer the discount, which averages about 21 percent. Originally, the pharmacies honored ScriptSave cards as a competitive advantage, but now, with some 50,000 pharmacies, including most of the major chains, accepting the card, it's become a requirement (and a cost of doing business).
- Drug manufacturers, which offer additional discounts to cardholders in order to gain market share.
- Seniors themselves, the ultimate customers, who reap the benefits of the discount card program.

To support the program, Horn has built a strong customer service organization, of which he is justifiably proud. He has used Stephen Covey's philosophy and training system[2] to build his corporate culture and achieve impressive results: 95 percent of customer calls answered in person within 15 seconds, one of the lowest "call abandonment" (customer hang-up) rates in the industry, an employee turnover rate less than half the industry average, and inclusion in the *Inc.* 500 list of fastest-growing companies three years in a row.[3]

- -

SCRIPTSAVE

Years in business:	12 (founded in 1994)
Start-up capital:	$100,000
Annual sales (2005):	$30 million
Corporate form:	Private for-profit
Business:	Prescription drug benefits

- -

So far, so good. Lots of little morphs have contributed to ScriptSave's success so far, but the big morph was scheduled to blow into ScriptSave's Tucson headquarters in January 2006, when the federal government was to begin offering its own prescription discount card for seniors.

End of ScriptSave, right?

Wrong.

On that site, the group eventually built the 64,000-square-foot Phillips Eco-Enterprise Center, a model of green building, which houses a mix of for-profit and nonprofit entities. In addition to providing a home for the Green Institute, which occupies only about 3 percent of the square footage, it generates revenue for the organization and jobs for neighborhood residents. Most recently, the institute has spawned a new consulting venture, the Green Buildings program, to sell the knowledge it gained through construction of the center.

But even before the group built the Eco-Enterprise Center, it was pioneering the field of green community development. Its flagship programs are the ReUse Center, a retail outlet for salvaged, reusable building materials, and DeConstruction Services, an enterprise that serves the building industry and supplies the ReUse Center. Today, the combined operation generates over $1 million a year in revenues and provides 18 living-wage jobs to community residents.[7]

Other environmentally oriented programs include the Community Energy Program, which focuses on both supply (generation of solar and biomass heat and power) and demand (conservation and energy efficiency), and GreenSpace Partners, which provides knowledge and services in the areas of stormwater management, green roofs, and community green spaces. All told, the Green Institute's continually morphing portfolio of projects now generates over $10 million a year in revenues and employs 25 people.[8]

But its most ambitious undertaking is just getting under way: the development of a $60 million biomass project serving a community energy district.

We're purchasing a site from the city that has an old garbage incinerator on it, and pretty much gutting the building and putting new modern technology in there that will burn wood waste and agricultural byproduct and generate electricity. Then we're increasing the efficiency by capturing the hot water from the electrical generation process and setting up a district energy loop that will serve about a one-mile stretch of commercial corridor.

There's been some federal funding, some state funding, some grant support, some funding from a utility program. That's going to be about $4 million when all is said and done. And then the balance of it will just come from traditional financing sources for power plants.

We haven't created any for-profit subsidiaries until now . . . but we're anticipating that [one we just created] will be the ownership structure for the power plant. One of the reasons for doing that is that there are some very attractive tax credits for energy projects. . . . So one of the things we're trying to figure out is how we can have a partnership with a private for-profit entity, kind of an equity partner, and allocate to them those tax losses as the primary source of return.[9]

This is a level of sophistication and scale that is well beyond the reach of most neighborhood activist groups, but the Green Institute didn't get there overnight. It morphed its way there over 12 years.

Flexcar

Flexcar, an American company based on the European idea of car sharing, has had to reinvent itself continually in order to get to a business model that will scale in multiple U.S. markets.

The company actually began with a 1999 request for proposal from King County Metro, which runs the Seattle bus system and was trying to promote car sharing as an extension of the public transportation system. Neil Peterson, who had previously been the head of Metro, decided to bid on the proposal. Flexcar was launched in January 2000.

FLEXCAR
Years in business: 6 (founded in 2000)
Start-up capital: NA
Annual sales (2005):   NA
Corporate form: Private for-profit
Business: Car sharing

Lance Ayrault, the firm's second CEO and president, was brought into the company in late 2002 to manage its rapid growth and refine its business model.

> The original pricing models on car-sharing companies in Europe and the United States were based on low hourly rates and high mileage rates. The academic portion of car sharing would say, "Make people pay for their actual usage and they'll be more inclined to use the cars efficiently. Your overall objective is to reduce the time people spend driving around in cars. They'll always take cars for what they need cars for and they're willing to pay for it."
>
> That's a great hypothesis, but the early data showed that people were taking these cars for the entire day because they're only $2 or $2.50 an hour, and they weren't driving anywhere. So at the end of the day, they'd get a car dedicated, sitting out in front of their house, that cost them ten bucks. Well, the company is going to go out of business pretty quickly under that model. You just can't make something like that work.
>
> So we basically turned that whole thing around and said, "Forget about the mileage charge," much to the chagrin of most of the academics who were looking at car sharing, who said, "How can you do that? Our mission is to reduce the amount of driving that goes on."
>
> I'm saying our mission is to get our cars driving all the time. That's what we're all about. And in doing that, there

will be all kinds of benefits. If I can get somebody out of an old beater into a low-emission vehicle, I'm helping the environment. If I can get a couple of people to leave their cars at home, I'm helping congestion. If I can get a business to get rid of 10 fleet cars and move into the Flexcar fleet, I'm saving parking space.

I think the way we should think about growing with our current model is probably more like hotel rooms or airline seats than anything else. Primarily what we're selling is availability of a car, and any hour that goes by that that car's not used is lost opportunity for us. So we've got to fill the capacity constantly.[10]

But refining the business model through experimentation and analysis was only half the battle. Ayrault also faced the classic chicken-and-egg dilemma that confronts innovators in the development of many new markets.

Our business is all about scale. So we've had a constant battle between the need to create the infrastructure in order to generate sales and the fact that if you put too much money into the infrastructure itself, you'll go bankrupt quickly, because you've got the infrastructure and you don't have the business.

I was talking the other day with a friend who said that the Flexcar model on a smaller scale is very much akin to what happened to Federal Express, where they were essentially bankrupt three or four different times as they were trying to get started up. What you needed was this massive infrastructure, and once you had it all in place, then it made sense for people to use it, and they were there just in time as people's habits were changing.

I think Flexcar is [in] the same situation. You need a network of cars that are pretty densely packed, you need a lot of cars, so that costs money. And if you put those cars out there before there's demand on those cars, they're very expensive for you.[11]

One of the best ways out of that dilemma is to find a partner with deep pockets who can make the up-front investment required for the market to take off. In Ayrault's case, the partner found him. In late May 2005, he got a call from AOL cofounder Steve Case, who expressed interest in the company. Three months later, the deal was done: Case's new investment firm, Revolution, bought the controlling interest in Flexcar and announced that Lee Iacocca would become a senior advisor to the firm.

The press release announcing the acquisition also outlined some of Case's immediate plans to scale up the enterprise: an increase in fleet size of more than 50 percent in three markets in the first 100 days, and expansion to at least six new metropolitan markets in the next year. And those were just the opening volleys in Flexcar's bid to "become the first truly national car-sharing firm."[12]

Case's purchase of Flexcar is totally consistent with the announced intentions of his new investment firm, Revolution. What is not clear is whether his interests are purely idiosyncratic or presage a new interest on the part of mainstream investors in helping a certain class of mission-driven ventures go to scale. If he is successful, others will certainly follow. In the meantime, his rhetoric is certainly inspiring:

> Many industries are on the brink of disruptive change, and we aim to build insurgent companies to capitalize on the emerging opportunities. . . .
>
> The best entrepreneurs have the best dreams—our focus is on turning them into reality. We partner with passionate entrepreneurs who are the architects of revolutionary change. We believe many companies ripe for breakthrough success already exist and we provide them the resources, insights, and muscle necessary to flourish. . . .
>
> We seek to build the leading brands in each sector we target, so we can achieve broad, mainstream appeal. . . . Revolution is about working closely with entrepreneurs to build

very significant companies that can truly revolutionize their industries. We don't just aim for a return—we seek to make history.[13]

■■LESSONS LEARNED

To me, the upshot of these three examples is a validation of the motto with which this chapter began: Faster learning beats better planning. This is not so much a case *against* planning as it is a case *for* improvisation. There are lessons to be learned from mixing it up in the marketplace that simply cannot be gleaned from market research and spreadsheet modeling.

And almost every business experiences a tension between sticking to the plan and pursuing unexpected opportunities as they present themselves. If you keep your head down and stick to the plan, you can easily miss important market data that would lead to good refinements of the plan, as well as new opportunities that might dwarf the original idea. On the other hand, if you simply abandon the plan to chase after every new opportunity that comes your way, you'll never succeed in bringing anything to scale.

The answer clearly lies somewhere in between. Three principles can help mission-driven firms to strike the right balance:

An unwavering commitment to mission

This provides a coherent theme for the organization's activities, the stable base upon which to improvise. It is an arena in which mission-driven firms have an advantage over their financially driven counterparts. When the mission is simply to make money, all things are possible, and it's very easy to get distracted. With a clear focus on mission—and a limited amount of cash—that is far less likely to happen.

Periodic reviews of the plan

The appropriate interval will vary from one business to the next, but the idea of regular reviews is important. It keeps the organization on track in the short term, while providing formal opportunities to reexamine core assumptions in the light of experience. This is particularly important as an organization attempts to go to scale. Reality is *always* different than plan—the question is, why? Regular reviews provide an opportunity to consider that question and make appropriate midcourse corrections.

The ability to manage small experiments

This enables the organization to innovate and learn from experience without making wholesale adjustments every time a new idea comes into view. If the experiments are successful, they can be rolled out in the rest of the organization. If they are unsuccessful, they won't sink the whole ship. And if they are somewhere in between, they afford the organization a great opportunity to do some significant "faster learning." ■ ■

CHAPTER EIGHT

Form Follows Function

MISSION-DRIVEN VENTURES come in all different flavors: for-profit, nonprofit, hybrid, public, private, co-op, employee stock ownership programs (ESOPs), community development corporations (CDCs), and forms that have yet to be invented. Each has advantages and disadvantages, but any corporate form can support a mission focus—even the much-maligned public corporation.

I have found a fair amount of "form envy" on both sides of the nonprofit/for-profit divide. Nonprofit practitioners are envious of the access to capital that their for-profit colleagues enjoy. For-profit practitioners are jealous of the nonprofits' tax-exempt status and access to donations. If you are starting from scratch, the critical question has to do with the long-term operating model for the business. If the goal is to get to breakeven or better on operating expenses, it probably makes sense to go the for-profit route because it offers more flexibility and access to capital. If you believe that your business model will always require some subsidization from donors, you probably need to set up the organization as a nonprofit. But that's a bit of layman's advice; an attorney needs to help you make the final determination.

J. Gregory Dees and Jed Emerson, two pioneers in the field of social enterprise, have done some of the best thinking on the topic of corporate form, particularly in their work on "blended value" and "for benefit" organizations.[1] The continuum below is roughly based on their work, combined with my own.

Continuum of Organizational Forms

By definition, none of the businesses I researched fell at either end of the spectrum. All were explicitly committed to delivering both social and financial returns. Still, they all have a place on this continuum, and it may be useful to explore the issues of corporate form by considering examples from left to right.

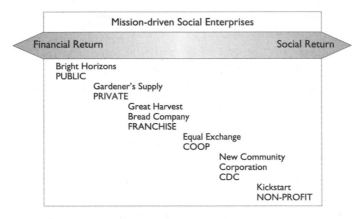

Examples of Organizational Forms

Bright Horizons Family Solutions Inc.

Both the critics and the defenders of the publicly traded corporation would be likely to agree on at least one thing: this is the organizational form *least* supportive of a focus on mission. That is because of the doctrine of shareholder primacy, which holds that the firm is owned by the shareholders and has a primary goal of maximizing their financial return on investment. The board works for the shareholders; the executive team works for the board; and everyone else works for the executive team. From top to bottom, the goal is to maximize the return to shareholders, and the enforcement mechanisms range from shareholder lawsuits to reductions in executive compensation to outright dismissal. Conversations about social returns tend to be confined to the PR department.

And yet, Bright Horizons, a purveyor of corporate-subsidized child-care centers, has done the impossible: it has fulfilled a complex social mission using venture capital funds for start-up and the public market for growth and liquidity.

■ ■

BRIGHT HORIZONS FAMILY SOLUTIONS INC.

Years in business:	20 (founded in 1986)
Start-up capital:	$2 million
Annual sales (2005):	$625 million
Corporate form:	Public for-profit
Business:	Child care

■ ■

The company was started in 1986 by the husband-and-wife team of Roger Brown and Linda Mason, who met at the Yale School of Management and spent their first years together working on large-scale refugee-relief operations in Cambodia and Sudan, and on the border of Ethiopia. When they returned to the United States, they spent some time figuring out what to do next, found themselves drawn to the child-care field, and shortly confronted the problem that they would turn into an opportunity. As Mason told the story,

> Once we started looking into the issue in greater depth, we realized there was a massive sociological revolution happening in our lifetime—the entrance of mothers of young children into the workforce. Clearly this meant an increase in demand for child care, yet the supply was not growing at all, and the large majority of child care that existed in our country was very poor in quality.
>
> We realized [that] the reason is that the economics of a single center really don't work. That's because of the intensive ratios: you need a teacher for every three babies. And to pay those teachers a good wage means the tuition is extremely high, and you have a situation that either the teachers are well paid and no one can afford the care, or if you make the care affordable, it puts tremendous downward pressure on wages.
>
> The only way it works is if there is a significant subsidy that comes in. So we thought, OK, we need a third-party subsidizer. And we looked at the changing demographics and the entrance of this enormous number of mothers going into the workplace, and we thought that perhaps the employer could provide this subsidy that would provide high-quality care. That perhaps it would be in the employer's best interest to have a high-quality child-care center on the site as a benefit for their employees to attract and retain good workers. So we came up with the concept of Bright Horizons: high-quality child care at the work site supported financially by the employer.[2]

In retrospect, this all seems obvious, but in 1986—and for 11 years thereafter—it was an idea ahead of its time. The company had difficulty finding its market—or, rather, waiting for its market to discover that it had the problem to which Bright Horizons had the solution—but it had little trouble financing its efforts and its mission.

> The first thing we did before we started the company was draw up a set of organizational values and a mission statement. So it was clear to anyone getting involved with us—an investor or a potential employee—what we stood for. When we met with potential investors, we described our quality model, our values, and our backgrounds in social service. So it was clear up front what investors were investing in. It didn't take us long at all to raise the capital.
>
> When we went public, that gave us an even greater opportunity to express our values. We took the company on a road show, and the first part of our presentation was on our mission and values. So it has always been front and center to what we do.
>
> And then, of course, once we were public, it gave us an even greater possibility to really talk about who we are and what we stand for. Once the business model makes sense, though—that helps a great deal.[3]

When queried about the prevailing assumption that quarterly earnings pressures make it particularly difficult for public companies to maintain their nonfinancial goals, Mason said that had not been her experience.

> In fact, when we were first creating the company, we first thought we'd create it as a nonprofit because most of our work had been with nonprofits. [But] we couldn't find enough grant money or foundation money to create Bright Horizons as a nonprofit. So then we thought, "Well, maybe we'll raise private capital." And we thought, "Now, will this impact our quality mission?" We reflected on it, and we said, "There's no reason why the way you are organized legally has to determine your mission and what you stand for."

We've always run Bright Horizons in the same way we did
our nonprofit. We founded a nonprofit the same time we
founded Bright Horizons, a nonprofit called Horizons for
Homeless Children, where we provide child care for the
homeless. And that has grown and is thriving right along-
side Bright Horizons. We manage it the same way. We're
mission driven in both organizations, we're fiscally responsible in both organizations.

We always talk to our employees about how Bright Horizons' strength resides in standing firmly on two legs, achieving our profit goals and achieving our quality goals. If we
have one without the other, it will be an unstable organization. And achieving our profit goals is not an end in itself;
it's the means through which we reach our quality goals. We
use the analogy that you need to breathe to live, [but]
breathing is not an end in itself; it's a means by which you
can live to achieve your other personal goals.[4]

Gardener's Supply Company

Will Raap, of Vermont's Gardener's Supply, has the situation that
most mission-driven entrepreneurs would consider ideal: he's
the majority owner of a successful, privately held firm. This is
ideal because private ownership gives him access to all the traditional sources of business capital, and majority ownership gives
him the control he needs to maintain a focus on mission.

Or, rather, missions, plural. Raap's include commitments to
the following:

- His employees, to whom he eventually hopes to sell the
  business.
- His community, where he has led the restoration of a 700-
  acre floodplain called the Intervale into an internationally
  known exemplar of sustainable agriculture.
- His customers, millions of gardeners nationwide, who benefit from his commitment to quality and innovation.

■ The planet itself, which may begin to be healed by a more nurturing relationship with its gardener-stewards, not to mention the 8 percent of pretax profits that Gardener's Supply gives away each year to earth-friendly nonprofits.[5]

■ ■

GARDENER'S SUPPLY COMPANY

Years in business:	23 (founded in 1983)
Start-up capital:	NA
Annual sales (2005):	$60 million
Corporate form:	Private, for-profit
Business:	Gardening supplies

■ ■

But just because Raap's ownership structure matches the theoretical ideal does not mean his business life has been easy. It just means that it may not be any harder than the life of any other small-business owner—which is plenty hard enough.

His biggest current problem, as with most independent retailers today, is competition from big box stores.

The gardening business used to have little niches. There used to be a niche where you could really serve people with interesting, effective, smart, unique products, whether it's tools and equipment or plants and bulbs. In the last 15 to 20 years, Home Depot, Lowe's, Wal-Mart, Kmart, Martha Stewart, [and others] got better and better at providing products to serve the peak gardening demand, which happens in six to eight weeks during the garden season.

They got very smart and aggressive in going after that business, offering, first, cheap prices, but then increasingly good product, innovative product, interesting product, good-quality product. And they have such scale that it's very difficult for people like us to be able to compete with them from a price standpoint.

So how do you compete? You try to do it with service, with differentiated quality, with brand distinctiveness, etc. How we've been able to grow and stay in business is, I think, mostly related to focusing on a defined mission . . . trying to find the customer base that is attracted to and responsive to that mission, and then being innovative in product to serve those customers. The bigger you get, the harder it is to do that because your niches become more mainstream, [so] you're competing with people who are mainstream.[6]

There isn't a great answer to that problem, regardless of ownership. Nor is there a great answer to the problem of transferring ownership. After running Gardener's Supply for 20-plus years and leading the Intervale restoration effort for almost that long, Raap would really like to be spending more of his time working in Costa Rica and other countries in the developing world, showing them how the Intervale model might be applied in their communities.

He wants to sell more of his interest in Gardener's Supply to his employees, who already own 30 percent of the company through an ESOP. But he's stymied. The business doesn't generate sufficient margins to cover both its working capital requirements and the stock-purchase program required to move more deeply into employee ownership. Thus, the logical exit for an owner with his values—selling the business to its employees—may not be a practical option. He's still working on it.

Great Harvest Bread Company

The only thing I don't understand about the Great Harvest Bread Company model is why it hasn't been copied more widely. It's a franchise system (albeit an unusual one, as you'll see in a minute), and as such it combines the virtues of a small-is-beautiful locally owned operation with all the wisdom and scale of a national organization. And it does both within the context of a winning mission:

[B]e loose and have fun, bake phenomenal bread, run fast to help customers, create strong exciting bakeries, and give generously to others.[7]

■ ■

GREAT HARVEST BREAD COMPANY

Years in business:	30 (founded in 1976)
Start-up capital:	"A shoestring"
Annual sales (2005):	$80 million (systemwide)
Corporate form:	Franchise
Business:	Whole grain bread

■ ■

Laura and Pete Wakeman opened their first bakery in Great Falls, Montana, in 1976, and the first franchise was opened in nearby Kalispell two years later. In 1983, the Wakemans sold their first bakery and focused on the franchise system full time.

The Wakemans, who were honored by *Inc.* magazine for their uniquely sane and balanced approach to the entrepreneurial life,[8] have now moved on to the next phase of their lives, but the system they created as a "learning organization" lives on. Their playful spirit, and that of their worthy successor, Mike Ferretti, comes through in the company's description of its Freedom Franchise operation:

If you look at most franchises, they began when some smart person figured out a way to make some money in a business and then wrote that recipe down and began to invite others to copy what she or he had done. The great thing about these sorts of franchises is that they aren't very risky for the person joining the franchise. The business is, after all, proven. Most franchises of this variety require their owners to do things the headquarters way. That's because HQ knows it works and also because the franchisor is trying to build a national brand, the foundation of which is consistency.

The problem with this sort of franchise, if you're an entre-
preneur-type, is that they aren't very much fun. All the good
stuff about opening your own business—figuring out what
you want to offer and what color the walls will be—aren't
your decisions to make. They've already been made.

At the other end of things is starting up and running your
own Mom and Pop shop. There you have all the freedom in
the world to create this thing just the way you want, but
you're flying solo, with no one else to lean on. That's why so
many start-ups fail.

We're trying to find that middle ground between the
advantages of a traditional franchise and the fun of a let's-
do-it-all-ourselves start-up. Our philosophy is simple. Let's
create Mom and Pop whole-wheat bakeries where Mom and
Pop know what the heck they're doing![9]

Franchise owners get all kinds of help from headquarters and
their peers—training, recipes, marketing assistance, financial
benchmarks, operational assistance, you name it—but they
aren't told what to do. Not only are they allowed to decorate
their stores any way they like, but also they're not even required
to use the same bread recipes. After a one-year apprenticeship,
they're set free to run their own businesses any way they want,
and they're encouraged to share both successes and failures with
their fellow franchisees through a range of formal and informal
mechanisms so successful that the company was profiled again
by *Inc.* magazine as a model "learning organization."[10]

Equal Exchange Inc.

Cooperatives—worker owned, producer owned, buyer owned,
or consumer owned—are a values-based ownership structure.
They are groups of people with a shared economic interest who
work together to achieve their economic objectives.[11]

Equal Exchange, the oldest and largest for-profit Fair Trade
company in the United States, is organized as a worker-owned

cooperative. Its mission is "to build long-term trade partnerships that are economically just and environmentally sound, to foster mutually beneficial relations between farmers and consumers and to demonstrate, through our success, the contribution of worker cooperatives and Fair Trade to a more equitable, democratic, and sustainable world."[12]

So far, it is doing just that. Founded in 1986, the co-op achieved profitability three years later and has been profitable for 16 of the last 17 years.[13] Based on those profits, the co-op's board of directors has declared annual dividends averaging 5.1 percent for the organization's nonvoting investors, in addition to the profits that accrue to the worker-owners.

■ ■

EQUAL EXCHANGE INC.

Years in business:	20 (founded in 1986)
Start-up capital:	$100,000
Annual sales (2005):	$20.8 million
Corporate form:	Worker-owned cooperative
Business:	Fair Trade coffee

■ ■

Equal Exchange is an interesting model in a number of respects, but its separation of governance from investment is particularly important. Equal Exchange has two classes of stock: common stock, which is exclusively available to employees on a one-member/one-voting-share basis; and preferred stock, which is available to outside investors in the form of nonvoting shares. As of January 2006, the co-op had raised $3.8 million from outside investors who were satisfied with the historical 5 percent dividend as a financial return and eager to support the social returns of Fair Trade.

Stock in the co-op does not appreciate. Cofounder and co-CEO Rink Dickinson's share cost $2,000 when he and his partners started the business in 1986, and he would get $2,000 if he left and sold his share back to the co-op today. His stock has no speculative value and no appreciation potential. But the stock does entitle each co-op worker-owner to a prorated share of the annual profits, as well as expose him or her to a proportional financial loss in a bad year. Since 2001, the annual rate of return on the worker-owner investment has been over 25 percent. But its other value is equally important: an opportunity to make a living while making a difference.

At Equal Exchange, that difference is not just about making life better for coffee growers through Fair Trade prices and practices. It's also about creating a viable model of a worker-owned, worker-controlled company based on a firm rule of one worker/one vote. Workers are eligible for voting membership in the co-op one year after they join the company, and they are given educational opportunities throughout their employment to help them to make good decisions as owners. In keeping with the values of workplace democracy, the maximum pay differential from highest to lowest is just three to one.[14]

Clearly, this is not a business model for everyone. And in fact Dickinson's two original partners, Jonathan Rosenthal and Michael Rozyne, have left the company for other pursuits. But it remains rewarding for Dickinson, his co-executive director, Rob Everts, and the 65-plus other worker-owners, who continue to set new records for sales, production, and making a difference in the lives of their cooperative farmers.

New Community Corporation

New Community Corporation is the story of a phoenix rising from the ashes of the 1967 riots in Newark, New Jersey. In the wake of that disaster, which left 26 people dead, 1,000 injured, and 1,600 arrested, as well as property damage totaling $15 million,[15] a young parish priest named Rev. William Linder founded a nonprofit organization to rebuild the city and "help residents of inner cities improve the quality of their lives to reflect individual God-given dignity and personal achievement."[16]

■ ■

NEW COMMUNITY CORPORATION

Years in business:	39 (founded in 1967)
Start-up capital:	NA
Annual sales (2005):	NA
Corporate form:	Community-development corporation
Business:	Housing, health care, education, job training and placement, manufacturing

■ ■

Today, nearly 40 years later, Father Linder is Monsignor Linder, and the organization he founded has assets of $500 million and programs and services that touch the lives of 50,000 residents of Newark and Essex County every day. The New Community Corporation (NCC) owns and manages 3,000 units of housing and employs 2,300 people. It develops and manages real estate; runs schools, health-care facilities, and financial institutions; provides social services and job training and placement; and, until recently, owned the majority interest in the only grocery store serving its central-city neighborhood.[17] In case there was any doubt, NCC is living proof that nonprofits can be every bit as enterprising and ambitious as their for-profit counterparts.

According to Linder, he and his colleagues had a desire to implement a comprehensive community-rebuilding effort from the beginning. But their resources were limited, so they began with the development of a small low-income housing project on a two-acre parcel. From there, they expanded dramatically, guided by two criteria: need in the community and the potential for job creation.

We chose to manage our own properties, to maintain our own properties, and to be the security of our own properties. Those three operations started as soon as we opened the housing. So we really began to have a more comprehensive view of where we wanted to go economically. We wanted to control those jobs so we could make them available locally [and] have a much more user-friendly system of training. For example, in environmental services or maintenance, we were able to train people for those jobs. And that was from day one. We spent a great deal of effort in the early days, really, getting people to take programs, go to school, and so on.

So we had the opportunity. And then we began to look and pick what the needs were. From day one, early-childhood [care] was needed [and] it was also very labor intensive. So we had Babyland Nursery, which eventually became a $15 million-a-year operation itself that took care of early childhood. And they started providing infant care—in fact, it was the first infant-care center in New Jersey. One of the reasons for it was that the ratios at that time were five infants to an adult, and that creates jobs.

The next thing we went into was health. And actually, health is now bigger than housing. And we had a home health-care program, which was good, because in a month or six weeks you can train someone and you give them the test yourself, you certify them, and it's recognized by the state.

And then, at the urging of our leaders, we went into senior housing. They wanted the nursing homes because they're all on Medicaid. So we went into that. And that's another one that produced . . . for a 180-bed nursing home, that's 275 jobs. And most of them, the vast majority, are not skilled. You do have nurses and RNs, but we have a lot more LPNs [licensed practical nurses], unlike a hospital. It was very labor intensive.

We began to expand the home health-care program. . . . We're putting a lot more time into training and health care, to the point we now train our own LPNs. Most of them that are going through the program now—we're on our fourth class—are former welfare recipients who have moved from that to home health care or certified nursing assistants, and then move from that to an LPN program. And hopefully in September [2005] we're going to be launching . . . an RN program.

We're trying to tie the economic opportunities, the intensity of labor that's needed, and the population that's here to get beyond just a living—at the same time meeting real service needs.[18]

One of the biggest obstacles nonprofits have to overcome to take their programs to scale is the ability to raise capital to fund their efforts. Although the burgeoning social-enterprise movement is attempting to point more of the nonprofit sector toward earned-income strategies, most nonprofits are still heavily dependent on grants and donations to achieve their social missions. New Community Corporation has taken a different tack.

We're very big on borrowing; actually, we have huge debt. And that has always been our strategy from day one—that it was more important to borrow than to get grants. And the reason is, I think, because there's a limited amount of grants, whether they be federal or private foundations. But borrowing is kind of unlimited. Once you can demonstrate you have the cash flow and you have sufficient reserves in one form or another, you're going to do pretty well.[19]

But even more than borrowing, what distinguishes the financing of NCC is its cleverness, drive, and sophistication. Every social problem seems to represent a business opportunity to NCC, and every newspaper article seems to contain a lead for bringing those opportunities to life. One article, in which the president of Hartz Mountain, the pet-products company, mentioned his interest in helping the homeless, led to a call from NCC's director of development, Ray Codey.

Our pitch to him . . . was that your headquarters are in New Jersey. You can help homeless people right here. He came

to see what we were doing. It turned out he was born on
the site of our nursing home. That's karma.[20]

KickStart

Perhaps the ultimate social-entrepreneurial model is that of a
nonprofit organization called KickStart (formerly ApproTEC),
which has developed a business model for lifting people out of
poverty one entrepreneurial family at a time. From an organizational standpoint, it is a unique hybrid.

■ ■

KICKSTART

Years in business:	15 (founded in 1991)
Start-up capital:	NA
Annual sales (2005):	$500,000 (700 pumps per month)
Corporate form:	Nonprofit
Business:	Technology transfer

■ ■

The parent organization, KickStart, is a nonprofit that raises
donor funds and contract funds to develop technologies, business models, and supply chains in the developing world, primarily (so far) in Africa. Its best-selling product is a very
low-tech irrigation pump that comes in two versions: the Super
MoneyMaker Pump, which costs $173 and irrigates two acres of
land, and the MoneyMaker Plus Pump, which costs $62 and
irrigates one acre. According to KickStart cofounder Martin
Fisher,

> On average, when people start using our pumps, they
> increase their net farm income by a factor of 10, from about
> $110 or $120 a year to $1,100–$1,200 a year. And this liter-
> ally lifts them from below the poverty line into the middle
> class. They can afford to send their kids to school, they can
> afford health care, they can afford to build houses. Already,

5,000 of them have actually spent their money to build houses; 50,000 kids are in school for the first time; we've got 39,000 operating businesses. And the total revenues they generate are equivalent to over 0.5 percent of GDP in Kenya and 0.25 percent in Tanzania. So they're having a huge national impact.[21]

What is at least as important as the impact on the lives of the individual families who make the investment in a pump is the larger business model that KickStart puts in place.

We basically plan to stay in the game until we reach a tipping point in a particular market. Where is that? Well, maybe that's 20 percent of market potential; we don't really know. But at some point, all of a sudden everybody becomes aware of these things. Everybody knows that, hey, this is an irrigation pump; it's not a magic little machine. The water is coming through this pump. And yes, I can buy one of these things and I can make money. And yes, I can get it repaired. And yes, there are people in town who know how to fix it and are selling them.

And then of course your marketing costs come way down. We use our donor funds to finance that initial market development. And then we leave in place a completely profitable, sustainable supply chain, where even we will make money on every sale.

So the manufacturer, the retailers, and KickStart all make money from every sale. Now, once we reach a tipping point in any particular marketplace with any given technology, it is completely sustainable and we also have a revenue stream, which we will then of course invest in expansion to other places. However, even then it will be a fairly small revenue stream. You don't get rich selling big-ticket items to poor people in developing countries. If you did, we wouldn't have to be here—people would have done it before.[22]

To date, KickStart has achieved the majority of its success in Kenya with its MoneyMaker line of irrigation pumps. But Kick-Start has begun to expand both its product line and market focus. Other products include a machine for making low-cost bricks from soil and cement, a machine for making cooking oil out of sunflower seeds, a manual hay baler, and a low-cost pit latrine. Products are now being sold in Tanzania and Mali, and the group is raising money to take its model into as many as four more countries over the next three years.

Scale has to be what it's all about. If we're not talking about scale, we're not talking about solving the world's problems. So it's fundamental to everything we do. When you want to take something to scale, you have to simplify it—distill your model down to a few simple rules. Because then it becomes something that you can take to a new location to replicate. You're no longer dependent on a particular charismatic leader; you're not dependent on local economic or social issues and conditions or particular government leaders.

And when you are evaluating any kind of social enterprise, there are only four questions you really have to ask: Does it have measurable proven impacts? Are the impacts extremely cost-effective? Will the impacts be sustainable when we leave? And can it be replicated and taken to scale? Because other-wise you shouldn't be spending donor funds if you cannot honestly answer yes to all four of those questions.

And then I always recommend that you start something with the low-hanging fruit. You start in an easy place. Some-body will usually say, "Well, I want to do something and then take it to the hardest place in the world. We're going to go where the need is the biggest." Well, that's great, but if you want to take something to scale, the vast majority of people actually don't live in the very worst places in the world. Let's take it to the low-hanging fruit and find the place where we can actually develop a model and make it work. Then you refine it, and then you distill it, and then you start saying, "OK, now we can start taking this to slightly harder places."[23]

■■LESSONS LEARNED

My take-away from these examples and all the companies I interviewed for this book is, "Where there's a will, there's a way." That is, if the commitment to mission is strong, it can be supported by any corporate form. Nonetheless, each form has its advantages and disadvantages. Some of the most prominent are summarized in the table below.

	Advantages	Disadvantages
Public corporation	■ Access to capital ■ Liquidity ■ Upside potential	■ Loss of control ■ Investor expectations make it difficult to maintain mission focus ■ Heavy costs of legal compliance and reporting
Private company	■ Owner control ■ Access to capital	■ Lack of liquidity ■ Outside investors may make it difficult to maintain mission focus
Franchise	■ Scales well ■ Local ownership ■ Requires capital in smaller chunks for easier financing	■ Applications limited to well-defined situations ■ Primarily retail or local service businesses
Cooperative	■ Structured to support members and their goals (e.g., agricultural producers, independent retailers) ■ Reduces costs; eliminates middlemen	■ Problematic access to capital ■ Limited upside potential ■ Governance can be cumbersome
Nonprofit	■ Mission focus is primary ■ Eligible for grants and donations ■ Favorable tax treatment	■ Limited access to capital ■ May lack business skills and entrepreneurial culture

ADVANTAGES AND DISADVANTAGES
OF ORGANIZATIONAL FORMS

CHAPTER NINE

The Soft Stuff
Is the Hardest

THE "SOFT STUFF" IN BUSINESS—the people side of things—
is almost invariably both the most difficult and the most important part of the equation. This is true regardless of whether the
firm is driven by money or by mission.

The people side of things is a two-edged sword in a mission-
driven business. On the one hand, values-based businesses are,
by definition, engaged in work that has a larger purpose, and
thus they are able to tap into a level of employee energy and
commitment that their profit-driven counterparts cannot fully
access. This commitment frequently translates into financial benefits for the organization, including lower labor costs, reduced
turnover, easier recruiting, higher attendance, and better morale
and performance.

On the other hand, mission-driven businesses tend to be held to
a higher standard than their financially driven counterparts. This
can create employee expectations that are difficult to fulfill in light
of business realities, and many employees—especially those who
are younger and less experienced—feel betrayed when the mission-driven firm doesn't live up to its espoused values. In a close-
knit, values-based firm, it can be especially hard to fire people who
share the firm's values but fail to meet its performance requirements. There is an ongoing challenge of walking the talk on issues
around work-life balance, "sustainable" hours and compensation,
participatory management, organizational transparency, and a host
of other internal commitments that tend to parallel the mission-
driven firm's commitments to the outside world.

All these issues fall in the realm of organizational culture, which most of the companies I interviewed agreed was both the most important and the most difficult aspect of getting to scale. Here are a few representative stories from companies you have already encountered in the course of this book—and a cautionary tale from one you haven't.

Bright Horizons Family Solutions Inc.

Bright Horizons is the publicly traded child-care company that manages corporate-sponsored, on-site child-care centers. Culture is the glue that holds together the firm's entire business model, from serving children and families to creating a professional environment for child-care workers to delivering financial returns to shareholders. According to cofounder and board chairman Linda Mason,

> Our greatest asset, without a doubt, is our internal culture. We have an incredibly strong internal culture, a real sense of mission. And people join us to be part of this culture and mission.
>
> Initially, the culture revolved largely around Roger and me, who we were, what we stood for. But then we very passionately and carefully hired managers and other senior leaders who also embodied this commitment to quality and this passion. Then they went on and they hired the same kind of people. It is such a part of who we are now, that if all the senior managers got run over by a truck tomorrow, the strong culture would continue, without a doubt.
>
> It starts with the hiring process. To be hired by Bright Horizons, you go through many interviews, and that in itself is culture building. Then it goes into the mentoring and orientation process, which is very much a sharing of our practices and our culture. And after orientation, it's an ongoing mentoring process.

It's in the environment. At your interview, you walk into a Bright Horizons center, and it's a very nurturing and respectful environment. It's also layered into the evaluation procedures: you're evaluated on personal qualities, the qualities of integrity and respect, as much as your [performance]. So it's layered in multiple areas of the organization.[1]

Equal Exchange Inc.

For Equal Exchange, the worker-owned coffee cooperative, managing corporate culture during a time of rapid growth was one of the key issues. Cofounder/co-CEO Rink Dickinson said,

> I think the challenge of scale is culture. It's about the issue of helping people to grow their skills as fast as the organization grows its sales. The three of us that started all had a pretty clear sense of what the mission was and were willing to do almost anything to try to make that work. How do you reproduce that culture? And how do you change that culture, because there are a lot of things that need to change as you go from 3 people to 10 people, and bring in another 7 people in a way that's healthy and effective.
>
> And then how would you go from 10 to 20 with the same thing? Having lived through this a couple of times, I think when you go past 30 people, there's this tremendous change in your culture.[2]

Within the issue of maintaining the corporate culture, Dickinson, like Linda Mason, stresses the critical importance of hiring. At Equal Exchange, that means not just hiring a coworker, but hiring a new co-owner with full voting privileges. The cooperative uses a hiring-committee process, which it considers so important that it treats it as a proprietary source of competitive advantage. The other reason for taking hiring so seriously, Dickinson admitted, is that "we're really bad at firing people—we're horrible at it—so we have to do the hiring really well."[3]

Eileen Fisher Inc.

At Eileen Fisher, the women's-clothing company, culture is so important that the organization employs a chief culture officer, who is a member of the company's leadership team. In addition, a little over half of the company's one-page mission statement is devoted to describing its "Practice," which is to say, culture.

Chief culture officer Susan Schor described the company's culture as combining a focus on individual growth and well-being with teamwork and collaboration.

> We make decisions in a reflective, thoughtful way, always thinking, "Who else might we want to think about this with us." It's a very collaborative process. Eileen often jokes and says we really need to look at things eight times before it feels right.
>
> We're inspired by the energy of teamwork and collaboration. It's a deeper priority to us than efficiency. Of course this means that some decisions take additional time to process, but the end result is more dimensional and satisfying to the whole.
>
> Our concept of leadership is as a facilitating leadership. We engage a certain amount of hierarchy/structure in order to facilitate and define our work, but we work toward being hierarchical in a minimal way. It's challenging for linear thinkers and conceptual thinkers to be asked to partner, but we're much more excited about a holistic outcome and see the value of shared, diverse thinking. We've also made a commitment to enhance facilitating leadership through the efforts of our Leadership, Learning and Development team.
>
> But getting back to what's unique about our culture that relates to the bottom line is that we honor our people, practice, and product as deeply as profits. We go so far as to believe that by honoring people, practice, and product, that profits naturally follow.

We find that our best thinking comes from sharing together, bouncing ideas off one another, and working things through until they feel right. We care more about the quality and richness than we do about efficiency. [Our culture] allows people to grow; it engages them and allows them to really be excited about their work.[4]

Seventh Generation Inc.

At Seventh Generation, CEO Jeffrey Hollender also stresses the importance of values and culture, but he has taken a more operational, nuts and bolts approach.

The first thing you have to do is articulate what that culture is, which is somewhat of a work in process. But you have to articulate it enough so that you can clearly explain to someone else what it is you're trying to create, what behaviors are and are not appropriate for that type of community environment.

Most people don't spend enough time articulating anything beyond the mission statement or the operating principles. That often doesn't give people enough information. We [have defined] those values out to the behaviors that are appropriate, and then we have further articulated the metrics that we are going to use to determine if our behavior is in keeping with those values.

This is in no way a replacement for individual performance plans and evaluations or financial evaluation. This is something that is done in addition to those things, but often integrated with them. So our performance plan will have personal growth objectives that are often directly linked to growth opportunities for people to behave more in keeping with our values. We don't segregate the need for someone to become a better listener or the need for someone to be more positive and less critical from the need for that person to achieve certain sales objectives or manage their budget.

We have what we call the "communication gap review," which doesn't have a very good name, but which really evaluates the departments and how they are doing in terms of their job and responsibilities—but, equally important, whether the department is functioning in keeping with the value system of the company. And now we are moving to the next horizon, which is external feedback from people outside the company, to see whether in fact their experience in doing business with us is an experience that is in keeping with what we say our values are.

You probably have to come back every couple of years to refresh that perspective to make sure that things haven't changed, because as the business grows and changes, my experience is that those values, some aspects of them, need to be fine-tuned.[5]

Frontier Natural Products Co-op: A Cautionary Tale

For most of my research, I picked companies with a strong track record of success and a founder who was still in the business and could tell me the story of how it grew to scale. Through a fluke, I met Andy Pauley, the board chair and CEO of Frontier Natural Products, a $50 million natural-foods business that was just emerging from hard times. Pauley was willing to share his story, which offers an interesting set of lessons about how *not* to manage corporate culture as a business attempts to get to scale.

■ ■

FRONTIER NATURAL PRODUCTS CO-OP

Years in business:	30 (founded in 1976)
Start-up capital:	"Founder's bank account"
Annual sales (2005):	$50 million
Corporate form:	Cooperative
Business:	Organic products, particularly herbs and spices, personal care, aromatherapy

■ ■

Frontier Natural Products started in 1976 outside of Cedar Rapids, Iowa, as a producer and consumer co-op. By 1999, which is when Pauley first became involved, it was still a co-op, doing a national business of about $40 million a year, primarily in organic herbs and spices and aromatherapy. Growth to that point had been organic—but the company had put in place a divisional organizational structure comparable to that found in companies four or five times its size.

> Management was looking at growing the business in distribution and manufacturing, the core strengths. Whereas the board group was [saying], "Gee, this company is organized in such a way and clearly has skill sets in such a way that we could be a much bigger company. We could double, triple in two to three years. How do we do that best? And is that a worthy goal?"
>
> Everyone at the board level [agreed] that what hadn't happened in the history of the company was taking advantage of the long-standing quality, integrity, and position that Frontier had in the industry. The great frustration of the CEO-founder for his last five years was . . . marketing. He knew it was a weakness, and he knew it was never going to come out of the Iowa culture. So he actually set up an office in Boulder, Colorado, and started hiring people into that office.[6]

The founder left the business shortly thereafter, and the newly formed board began to address those questions through a strategic planning process. At a critical juncture in that process, the Iowa-based, operations-oriented management team came up with a strategic direction based on the organization's historic core competencies; the board came up with a plan to build the organization's marketing skills to support more rapid growth. The board prevailed; the firm hired a marketing-savvy CEO, spun a couple of C corporations out of the co-op, and moved the corporate headquarters to Boulder.

The operations people—the people with all the history in the business and the tacit knowledge of how it worked—stayed in Iowa. The company failed to meet its product shipment goals, and then the finger-pointing began. The Boulder CEO blamed the people in Iowa and their "old-fashioned notion of what the organic movement is all about," and the Iowa people blamed the Boulder marketing types for not "paying enough attention to the people they needed to rely on to actually execute the strategy."

In the end, the operations people were right; the marketers were wrong. The board fired the CEO and his management team, closed the Boulder office, dropped a set of product launches, cut back expenses, and still barely escaped bankruptcy. The remainder of the company went back to Iowa—literally and figuratively—and has been in a turnaround situation ever since, under the direction of its board chair, Andy Pauley. He subsequently reported,

> Within the first year, the company had settled back into profitability and was continuing to work on its excess inventory based on some of the failed launches. Some product lines were sold off (boxed pasta to Annie's, for example) and some were completely discontinued. Block and tackle work of the core businesses guided the stability. The new board, which completely replaced the previous group, is primarily from the natural products sector and has assisted management in the quick turnaround.[7]

■■LESSONS LEARNED

I've told this last story at some length because it is so typical of traditional businesses and so atypical of the successful mission-driven entrepreneurs I interviewed. After 20 years of operating very much like the companies described in this book, Frontier tried to change its strategy, personnel, product line, market focus, growth rate, internal relations, corporate form, capitalization—you name it. All this was done in the name of opportunity and strategy, both of which were real, but not as easily realized as the new outside executive team thought. In retrospect, their plans look like hubris, but in prospect, they simply looked like the fast track for getting to scale. The fast track is seldom the right approach for the mission-driven firm, however.

The other examples were less about changing the culture to support growth and more about supporting the culture through the challenges of growth. Although each of the cultures was different—and each of the organizations took a different approach to maintaining the culture—there were definitely some common elements:

- The importance of *hiring* well from a cultural standpoint as well as a skills standpoint, particularly given the difficulty of firing.
- The need to continually *reinforce* the culture through as many mechanisms as possible, to walk the talk both formally and informally, and to include cultural elements in performance evaluations.
- The extent to which the founder and executive team spent time thinking about, working on, and transmitting the culture—in general, recognizing its *importance* in supporting the organization, its people, and its mission.

Throughout my conversations with the entrepreneurs I interviewed for this book, I was struck by their humility—an unexpected humility, given the healthy egos more generally characteristic of the breed. I think that a commitment to mission—particularly to a difficult, lofty mission not likely to be achieved in a single lifetime—breeds humility and leads in turn to an emphasis on transparency. Over and over again, I heard the equivalent of "This is where we're headed, but of course we're not there yet." That attitude, coupled with open-book management and a general practice of transparency, helped the entrepreneurs to manage expectations on the part of both customers and employees, keeping attitudes positive even when performance fell short of goal. ■■

CHAPTER TEN

Getting to Scale: Is It Right for You?

GETTING TO SCALE is not for everyone. This final chapter attempts to synthesize the lessons I've learned into a framework that can help mission-driven entrepreneurs evaluate the role of scale in their own business ventures. It is structured around three critical questions:

1. How do you define success?
2. How big do you need to be to succeed at your *mission*?
3. How big do you need to be to succeed at your *business*?

Defining Success

This is a very personal question, and one to which the answers change over time.

Entrepreneurs go into business for many reasons: to make a living, to support their families, to serve their communities, to gain control over their work lives, to challenge themselves, to make a lot of money, to make the world a better place.

Even within the narrower realm of mission-driven businesses, there are a number of different methods, motivations, and definitions of success. For many mission-driven entrepreneurs, scale is not an issue. In fact, growth beyond a certain point may be counterproductive to their values of localism and lifestyle. Growth comes at a price—in financial and organizational complexity, level of risk, and hours away from home and family— that many entrepreneurs are simply unwilling to pay.

It is also true that entrepreneurs may begin with one set of ambitions and end up with another. They may start off with a relatively modest set of goals, achieve success, and find that their ambitions have grown beyond their original expectations. Conversely, they may start off with huge ambitions and scale them back as reality sets in or their personal priorities change.

All of these answers—and more—are totally legitimate. What matters most is that you ask the question, and then ask it again as the business grows. It's also important not to ask it too frequently—like every time you hit a bump in the road. "Are we having fun yet?" is a more appropriate, lighthearted question for day-to-day setbacks. But "Am I doing the right thing?" and "Are we headed down the right path?" are questions that demand periodic reflection.

Succeeding at the Mission

This is the second line of inquiry for mission-driven firms, and, once again, I believe there are many possible answers. This is also a question that needs to be asked iteratively and in conjunction with the other two questions. How big must the business be to succeed at *your* mission in the world, and how big must the business be to survive and pursue *its* mission in the world?

Missions come in many sizes: community, industry, country, problem, region, planet. People who build mission-driven businesses may choose to play at any—or many—levels.

Most businesses start in a single physical location and expand from there. For financially driven businesses, the decision to grow is a result of the desire to grow profits, and "getting to scale" is about achieving scale economies that contribute to profits. For mission-driven businesses, the decision to grow is much more likely to be about extending social benefits beyond the original location. Getting to scale is thus about affecting the world on a broader basis.

This difference in motivation is critical. Since mission-driven entrepreneurs are generally not motivated by profit per se, they don't necessarily have to own every location where their model is in use. Thus, particularly in the realm of nonprofits, creating a model that can be replicated elsewhere may be a particularly attractive approach to getting to scale.[1] The model may simply be a successful example for others to copy on their own, or it may be part of a program-extension effort at the national or international level.

In some cases—David Green's Project Impact comes to mind—the goal may be to simply prove the viability of the market and pave the way for others, including for-profit ventures, to follow. What matters to him, and to others like him, is the results, not the distribution of profits. Even Jeff Mendelsohn, head of the for-profit New Leaf Paper, is primarily concerned with setting an example that will push the mainstream paper industry in a more sustainable direction. And Dal LaMagna, the founder of Tweezerman, wanted to get big enough to establish the viability of his brand of "responsible capitalism" as a serious business proposition.

Scale was critical to the fulfillment of mission in the case of the producer cooperatives profiled in this book. In those instances, the whole point of the business arrangement was to enable a bunch of independent farmers and ranchers to band together and get to scale in production and marketing, thereby giving them greater control over their destiny. In other cases, such as Will Raap's Gardener's Supply, scale was required to be able to offer employee benefits congruent with the company's values.

The point here is to recognize that the relationship between mission and scale varies from one situation to the next. There is no single right answer—just a continuing need to ask the question.

Succeeding at the Business

How big do you need to be to succeed at your business? This has been the question at the core of this book. What does it really mean to "get to scale"?

The first answer to that question is to recognize that getting to scale is a journey rather than a destination. In some ways, the subtitle of this book—"Growing Your Business without Selling Out"—may be a more accurate description of its content than the main title is. There is not necessarily a precise point, calculated with some sophisticated analytical model, at which a business arrives at "scale." But there are definitely some points on the growth curve of a business that are more comfortable, profitable, and capable of having the desired impact than others.

How do you find those points? As other authors have suggested,[2] I would begin by mapping the firm's value chain and then analyzing that chain in terms of the implications of scale. A fairly standard value chain might look something like this:

Raw materials	Production	Distribution	Marketing and sales	Customer

Standard Value Chain

To get a feel for how this might work, I'll use it to map four different mission-driven businesses: two product companies, Organic Valley Family of Farms and New Belgium Brewing Company; and two service companies, Novex Couriers and Bright Horizons Family Solutions, shown on the facing page.

The product companies

The mission of Organic Valley is to support dairy farmers by providing stable prices and markets for their products. Its value proposition to consumers is fresh, healthy, organic dairy products that support family farms. Scale issues are critical throughout its value chain. First, the co-op must try to match supply and demand, a challenge compounded by the perishability of its products. Second, it must manage processing, packaging, and inbound and outbound logistics—all the operations pieces

Organic Valley Family of Farms	New Belgium Brewing Co.	Novex Couriers	Bright Horizons Family Solutions
Raw materials Milk from organic family farms	Hops, malt, barley, wheat, etc.	Service providers: couriers (also cars, gas, etc.)	Service providers: child-care workers (also facilities)
Production Co-pack firms	Brewery	Routing	Curriculum, training, standard operating procedures
Distribution Trucks, warehouses	Trucks, warehouses	N/A	N/A
Marketing and sales Consumer and retailer	Consumer and retailer	Business	Business and consumer
Customer Shoppers	Drinkers	Businesses and professionals	Corporations

VALUE CHAIN ANALYSIS

of the business. Third, it must manage its marketing efforts to secure shelf space from grocers and mind share from consumers.

Once these requirements are understood, one way to approach them is as a classic "make versus buy" business decision—that is, as a question of whether Organic Valley should make capacity by building its own processing facilities and distribution network, or buy capacity from others through contracts. So far, it has made sense for Organic Valley to buy most of its capacity from others, partly because the co-op hasn't had the volume to justify its own plants and partly because it hasn't had the ability to finance that capital investment. As it grows, it will need to continually reevaluate this strategy. Its *mission* does not require it to own its facilities, but that may eventually make good business sense.

New Belgium Brewing Company, on the other hand, *does* own its own processing facility because its core business is production—in this case, the brewing of world-class Belgian-style beers. Because the company could not simply contract production capacity from others, it has had to grow its own—and is now in its third location and eighth expansion effort. Because brewing is an asset-intensive business, the owners of New Belgium have frequently had to build capacity ahead of sales—they haven't been able to simply add it on a pay-as-you-go basis. They have been lucky in being able to finance their growth through a combination of personal savings, business revenues, and bank loans—and therefore haven't had to give up any equity. But the kind of dramatic growth they've enjoyed, coupled with the capital-intensive nature of their industry, frequently requires a business to bring in outside investors, with all the corresponding threats to mission and independence.

In a consumer products company like New Belgium or Organic Valley, marketing is typically a huge expense and one that begs for economies of scale or scope.[3] But in both these cases—and most of the others reported in this book—a combination of product differentiation and marketing cleverness has had to substitute for a large marketing budget.

The service companies

Scale economies operate somewhat differently in service businesses but are still a major issue. At Novex Couriers, "plant capacity" is added one vehicle and one driver at a time, but capacity utilization—a fundamental scale issue—is the key to profitability. To put it simply, the costs of the car, the driver, and the ad in the yellow pages are all the same whether the car is on the road making deliveries and making money, or sitting in the parking lot waiting for a call. The fundamental idea behind economies of scale is the ability to spread fixed costs over higher volumes, and in a service business with full-time employees, salaries are basically a fixed expense—one that must be recovered by spreading it over a volume of work.

Equally significant are the marketing and selling expenses. It costs a business like Novex the same amount of money to run the ads, answer the phone, and make the sales calls whether it is dispatching 5 cars, 15 cars, or 50 cars. Part of the challenge, once again, is to match supply and demand: to do enough marketing to keep cars and couriers busy, but not so much that you have to turn customers down.

Bright Horizons Family Solutions, another service company, has yet another business model and yet another set of scale considerations. Its mission is to provide high-quality employer-sponsored child-care services, primarily on-site at large corporations. Bright Horizons markets its services to employers with a solid set of employee retention and productivity benefits. Its customers (the employers) bear the brunt of the capital costs of its business—building and maintaining the centers—and the families that Bright Horizons serves pick up the variable costs, with assistance from their employers. Because the staffing ratios required by law are so low (one caregiver to four or five infants or preschoolers), it is possible to match supply and demand fairly tightly. Thus, this is a very scalable business now that it is up and running.

These four examples underscore one of the basic messages of this book, which is that getting to scale is not a simple, one-size-fits-all imperative. It is a choice—or, more accurately, a series of choices. Here's a list of questions to help you think through those choices in your own company.

Analyzing the Impacts of Scale

Raw Materials

- ☐ What are the raw materials used in your business?
- ☐ Where do they come from? (Are they geographically restricted?)
- ☐ Are they heavy and/or bulky and expensive to ship and store?
- ☐ Are they perishable?
- ☐ Are there requirements for or advantages to purchasing them in bulk?

☐ Do prices and availability fluctuate, making it desirable to keep them in inventory?

☐ How important are any of these factors in determining cost structure—and pricing—in your business?

Production

☐ Do you have to own your own production facilities, or can you contract production services from others?

☐ If you can contract services from others, what is the cost per unit at various levels of volume?

☐ Is the supplier reliable in terms of quality and availability?

☐ What are the carrying costs of inventory?

☐ If you must own your own production facilities, how much will they cost to build or buy?

☐ Can you add capacity on a modular basis?

☐ Can you sell excess capacity to others?

☐ How can you finance production capacity? How much will you have to pay for that financing, in terms of both money and control?

☐ If you have a "make or buy" choice between building your own production capacity and/or buying capacity on contract from others, how do the costs and quality compare? Is the difference worth the risk and hassle of ownership?

Distribution

☐ How do raw materials get to the production facility? Who pays the freight?

☐ How do finished goods get to customers?

☐ Who are the middlemen in your distribution chain? What services do they perform?

☐ What are the costs of storing and managing inventory?

☐ To what extent are your distribution costs fixed or variable? How can they be made more variable?

☐ What percentage of your costs and/or the consumer's price is in distribution expenses? In other words, how important is distribution in your cost structure?

☐ If you have a choice between doing some of the distribution functions yourself or farming them out, what are the costs and benefits of each approach? What are the risks of each?

Marketing and Sales

☐ How is your product or service sold?

☐ What is the breakeven cost of adding a salesperson?

☐ Are there "economies of scope" in your sales approach, where a single call can be used to sell multiple products or services?

☐ What is the relationship between sales and distribution in your business, if any?

☐ How much of your marketing expense is fixed—that is, a required cost of doing business rather than a discretionary expense that can be ramped up or down?

☐ How much of an up-front investment in marketing do you need to make ahead of sales? How long will it take to realize the benefit of that investment? And how will you know if it's effective?

☐ What percentage of your costs and/or the consumer's price is in sales and marketing expenses? In other words, how important is this variable in the cost structure of your business and your industry?

☐ How can you leverage partnerships to reduce your costs for marketing and sales?

Bringing a mission-driven business to scale is incredibly challenging. But for those who choose to accept the challenge, the reward is also significant: a chance to make a bigger difference in the world—and to set an example for others. The entrepreneurs profiled in this book—and the many others who have also stepped up to the challenge—are living proof that there's a better, more socially useful way to do business than the one we've settled for in most of our economy. Once we understand how it works, there's no reason to do business any other way. ■ ■

Notes

Preface

1. Milton Friedman, "The Social Responsibility of Business Is to Increase Its Profits," *New York Times Magazine*, September 13, 1970.
2. Net Impact, www.netimpact.org (accessed March 27, 2006).

Introduction

1. Ben Cohen and Jerry Greenfield, *Ben & Jerry's Double-Dip: How to Run a Values-Led Business and Make Money, Too* (New York: Simon & Schuster, 1997).
2. Gary Hirschberg, telephone interview by David Korten, July 2003.
3. E. F. Schumaker, *Small Is Beautiful: Economics As If People Mattered* (New York: Harper & Row, 1973).
4. Michael Shuman, *Going Local: Creating Self-Reliant Communities in a Global Age* (New York: The Free Press, 1998).
5. Joseph Pine, *Mass Customization: The New Frontier in Business Competition* (Boston: Harvard Business School Press, 1999).
6. The definitive work on this topic, Alfred D. Chandler Jr.'s *Scale and Scope: The Dynamics of Industrial Capitalism* (Cambridge: Harvard University Press, 1990), distinguishes between economies of scale—"those that result when the increased size of a single operating unit producing or distributing a single product reduces the unit cost of production or distribution"—and economies of scope—"those resulting from the use of processes within a single operating unit to produce or distribute more than one product." While this distinction may be useful in some situations, I use the general term *economies of scale* to refer to all such instances.
7. For more on this topic, see Clayton M. Christensen's *The Innovator's Dilemma: When New Technologies Cause Great Firms to Fail* (Boston: Harvard Business School Press, 1997).
8. I am indebted to David Korten for this language and some of the thinking behind it.
9. Eureka Communities, case study of New Community Corporation, www.eureka-communities.org (accessed July 1, 2005). See also, New Community Corporation, www.newcommunity.org/.
10. Michael E. Porter, *Competitive Strategy: Techniques for Analyzing Industries and Competitors* (New York: The Free Press, 1980).
11. Ibid., p. 42.

12. The Social Venture Network is a nonprofit network organization that supports the efforts of its member mission-driven firms and strengthening of the social-enterprise sector in general. For further information, see www.svn.org.
13. The Co-op America Business Network is a larger, somewhat more diverse network of mission-driven businesses that are committed to using business as a tool for social change. For further information, see www.coopamerica.org.
14–17. In these three cases, I did not speak to the principals directly but relied on primary-source interviews conducted by others.

Chapter I. Mission Comes First

1. Interview with Laura Scher, May 9, 2005.
2. Interview with Sean Penrith, April 25, 2005.
3. Interview with George Siemon, March 22, 2005.
4. Interview with David Van Seters, June 14, 2005.
5. Ibid.
6. Ibid.
7. Ibid.
8. I am indebted to Lorinda Rowledge, Ph.D., my colleague at BGI, for helping me to understand this point. She calls the sweet spot the "nexus" and has written about it in *Mapping the Journey: Case Studies in Strategy and Action toward Sustainable Development,* coauthored with Russell S. Barton and Kevin S. Brady (Sheffield, England: Greenleaf Publishing, 1999).
9. SPUD, www.spud.ca (accessed March 27, 2006).

Chapter 2. Any Business Can Do It

1. Marjorie Kelly, "The Legacy Problem," *Business Ethics,* Summer 2003.
2. For more information, see the Social Venture Network Web site, www.svn.org.
3. Interview with Mark Deutschmann, May 10, 2005.
4. Village Real Estate Services, www.villagerealestate.com (accessed March 27, 2006).
5. Ibid.
6. Interview with Mark Deutschmann.
7. Interview with Rob Safrata, June 16, 2005.
8. Novex Couriers, www.novexclean.ca (accessed March 27, 2006).
9. Interview with Rob Safrata.
10. Ibid.
11. Ibid.
12. New Belgium Brewing Company, www.newbelgium.com (accessed March 27, 2006), and interview with Kim Jordan, January 11, 2005.

13. New Belgium Brewing Company, www.newbelgium.com.
14. "Wellth-in-Action: New Belgium Brewery," Wisdom Works Group, Inc., www.wisdom-works.net (accessed March 27, 2006).
15. Modern Brewery Age, June 9, 2003 (accessed on March 27, 2006 from www.findarticles.com).
16. W.K. Kellogg Foundation, "A Network of Innovators Pursues Triple Bottom Line," interview with Dal LaMagna, August 2003, http://wkkf.org (accessed March 27, 2006).
17. Thea Singer, "Strategies: Radical Sabbaticals," *Inc.*, August 2002.
18. A. J. Carter, "Getting Hands-on with Guacamole," *Newsday*, July 11, 2005.
19. Interview with Dal LaMagna, May 10, 2005.
20. New Belgium had no outside investors. Tweezerman had a small group of family members, friends, and business suppliers who owned the 10 percent of the stock not owned by the founder.
21. Wild Planet Toys, www.wildplanet.com (accessed March 27, 2006).
22. Interview with Jennifer Chapman, May 10, 2005.
23. Ibid.
24. Wild Planet Toys, www.wildplanet.com.
25. Interview with Jennifer Chapman.
26. Joe Eskenazi, "Toy with Me: From His First Chanukah, Daniel Grossman Was Hooked on Toys, but Now He Makes Them," *J. The Jewish news weekly of Northern California*, December 12, 2003.
27. Interview with Jennifer Chapman, May 10, 2005.

Chapter 3. Organic Is the Way to Grow

1. The mantra of the dot-com era, a phrase coined by Jeff Bezos of Amazon.com.
2. Organic Valley, www.organicvalley.coop (accessed March 27, 2006).
3. Ibid.
4. Organic Trade Association, www.ota.com (accessed March 27, 2006).
5. Cooperative Regions of Organic Producer Pools (CROPP), Offering Circular, June 14, 2004.
6. A reference to "Old MacDonald Had a Farm," in case you haven't been around any preschoolers lately.
7. Interview with George Siemon, March 22, 2005.
8. Correspondence with Sue McGovern, writer, January 10, 2006.
9. Ibid.
10. Professor Jules Pretty, "Rethinking Agri-Culture: As If the Real World Matters," Leopold Institute for Sustainable Agriculture, Iowa State University (www.leopold.iastate.edu), October 20, 2003 (accessed from Organic Valley, www.organicvalley.coop).
11. Interview with Margot Fraser, April 21, 2005.
12. Birkenstock, www.birkenstock.com (accessed August 5, 2005).
13. *MBA Jungle* magazine, May 27, 2004.

14. Interview with Margot Fraser, April 19, 2005.

15. Mary Scott and Howard Rothman, *Companies with a Conscience: Intimate Portraits of Twelve Firms That Make a Difference* (New York: Birch Lane Press, 1992).

16. Wayne Niemi, "Fraser Retakes the Reins: Two Years after Leaving Birkenstock USA as CEO, Well-Known Founder Is Back in the Driver's Seat," *Footwear News,* December 13, 2004.

17. Interview with Margot Fraser, April 19, 2005.

18. Wayne Niemi, "Birkenstock Footprint Sandals Is Slimming Down," *Footwear News,* October 17, 2005.

19. Interview with Jeffrey Hollender, April 1, 2005.

20. Ibid.

21. Organic Trade Association (OTA), "The Organic Industry Flyer," www.ota.com (accessed December 24, 2005).

22. This trend is sometimes referred to as the rise of the LOHAS (lifestyles of health and sustainability) market.

Chapter 4. Finance Your Independence

1. See Investors' Circle, www.investorscircle.net.

2. Interview with Kim Jordan, May 18, 2005.

3. Investors' Circle, www.investorscircle.net (accessed March 27, 2006).

4. Both available at RISE, www.riseproject.org.

5. Catherine Clark and Josie Taylor Gaillard, *RISE Capital Market Report: The Double Bottom Line Private Equity Landscape in 2002/2003,* page 11, www.riseproject.org.

6. New Energy Finance estimates that total global investment in clean energy (renewable energy plus low-carbon technologies) in 2005 will have been around $42.2 billion, which would dwarf the investment in all other double-bottom-line areas. Source: Clean Edge, www.cleanedge.com (accessed March 27, 2006).

7. Clark and Gaillard, op. cit., page 17.

8. Woody Tasch, "Slow Money," *More Than Money* magazine, August 2004.

9. Interview with Jason Finnis, March 1, 2005.

10. As of December 2005, the company had yet to make a profit, largely because it had chosen to fund its development of the Crailar technology out of operations. According to Finnis, the expenses associated with its public-ownership structure were another significant drain on profitability.

11. Interview with Jason Finnis, March 1, 2005.

12. AEA Investors, a private equity firm.

13. Interview with Tom McMakin, February 26, 2004.

14. Pura Vida Coffee, www.puravidacoffee.com (accessed December 26, 2005).

15. Interview with John Sage, May 19, 2005.

16. Pura Vida is a for-profit company owned by a public charity, Parity of Partners, that was set up by Sage and Dearnley.
17. Interview with John Sage, May 19, 2005.
18. Upstream 21, "Summary of Private Placement Offering." The offering closed December 31, 2005, with operations planned to begin in 2006.
19. Interview with Leslie Christian, September 17, 2004.
20. Articles of Incorporation of Upstream 21 Corporation.
21. Jim Collins, "Built to Flip," *Fast Company*, March 2000.
22. Interview with Dal LaMagna, May 10, 2005.

Chapter 5. Build Your Values into the Brand

1. Jacquelyn A. Ottman, *Green Marketing: Opportunity for Innovation* (NTC-McGraw-Hill, 1998). Available for free download at J. Ottman Consulting, Inc., www.greenmarketing.com.
2. Peter Donovan, "Oregon Country Beef: Growing a Solution to Economic, Environmental, and Social Needs—an Interview with Doc and Connie Hatfield," Managing Wholes, www.managingwholes.com (accessed March 27, 2006).
3. Country Natural Beef, www.oregoncountrybeef.com (accessed March 27, 2006).
4. Ibid.
5. Interview with Doc and Connie Hatfield, March 15, 2005.
6. Country Natural Beef, www.oregoncountrybeef.com (accessed July 18, 2005).
7. Interview with Doc and Connie Hatfield, March 15, 2005.
8. Ibid.
9. Eileen Fisher, Corporate press kit, April 2005.
10. Ibid.
11. After Paul Newman and his family of food products. Newman gives away 100 percent of the profits on sales of the Newman's Own line.
12. Interview with Mike Hannigan, "A Network of Innovators Pursues Triple Bottom Line," in "Kellogg Foundation Profiles SVN," Social Venture Network (SVN), www.svn.org, accessed November 12, 2005.
13. Ibid.
14. Ibid.

Chapter 6. Match Manufacturing to Mission

1. Ashoka (www.ashoka.org) identifies individual "social entrepreneurs" working on large-scale social-change efforts around the world and supports their efforts through its Ashoka Fellows program.
2. Ashoka, www.ashoka.org (accessed March 27, 2006).
3. See C. K. Prahalad, *The Fortune at the Bottom of the Pyramid* (New Jersey: Wharton School Publishing, 2005).

Chapter 9. The Soft Stuff Is the Hardest

1. Interview with Linda Mason, May 24, 2005.
2. Interview with Rink Dickinson, March 4, 2005.
3. Ibid.
4. Interview with Susan Schor, April 12, 2005.
5. Interview with Jeffrey Hollender, March 16, 2005.
6. Interview with Andy Pauley, February 24, 2005.
7. Correspondence from Andy Pauley, January 12, 2006.

Chapter 10. Getting to Scale: Is It Right for You?

1. See two articles in the *Stanford Social Innovation Review* for insights into this strategy: Jeffrey L. Bradach, "Replicating Social Programs," Spring 2003; and J. Gregory Dees, Beth Battle Anderson, and Jane Wei-Skillern, "Scaling Social Impact," Spring 2004.
2. Alex Kandybin, Martin Kihn, and Cesare R. Mainardi, "Reinventing Scale: How to Escape the Size Trap," *Strategy + Business*, Second Quarter, 2000.
3. "Economies of scope" refers to the idea of pushing multiple products (as opposed to larger volumes) through a single infrastructure—a single sales force, for example.

Additional Resources

Biographies and Autobiographies of Mission-driven Entrepreneurs

Abrams, John. *The Company We Keep: Reinventing Small Business for People, Community and Place.* White River Junction, VT: Chelsea Green Publishing, 2005. Founder and CEO of South Mountain Company, an employee-owned design/build firm on Martha's Vineyard.

Bakke, Dennis W. *Joy at Work: A Revolutionary Approach to Fun on the Job.* Seattle: PVG, 2005. Founder and former CEO of AES, a multi-billion-dollar international energy company.

Chappell, Tom. *The Soul of a Business: Managing for Profit and the Common Good.* New York: Bantam, 1996. Founder and CEO of Tom's of Maine.

Chouinard, Yvon. *Let My People Go Surfing: The Education of a Reluctant Businessman.* New York: Penguin Press, 2005. Founder and owner of Patagonia.

Cohen, Ben, and Jerry Greenfield. *Ben & Jerry's Double Dip: How to Run a Values-Led Business and Make a Profit, Too.* New York: Simon & Schuster, 1997. Cofounders of Ben & Jerry's Ice Cream.

Erickson, Gary, with Lois Lorentzen. *Raising the Bar: Integrity and Passion in Life and Business: The Story of Clif Bar Inc.* San Francisco: Jossey-Bass, 2004. Founder and former CEO of Clif Bar.

Lager, Fred. *Ben & Jerry's: The Inside Scoop: How Two Real Guys Built a Business with a Social Conscience and a Sense of Humor.* New York: Three Rivers Press, 1995 (reprint edition). An early employee and later CEO of Ben & Jerry's.

McMakin, Tom. *Bread and Butter: What a Bunch of Bakers Taught Me about Business and Happiness.* New York: St. Martin's Press, 2001. Former CEO of Great Harvest Bread Company.

Roddick, Anita. *Body and Soul: Profits with Principles—The Amazing Success Story of Anita Roddick & The Body Shop.* New York: Three Rivers Press, 1994 (reissue edition). Founder of The Body Shop.

Roddick, Anita. *Business as Unusual: The Triumph of Anita Roddick.* London: Thorsons Publishers, 2001. Founder of The Body Shop.

Rosenzweig, Bill, Mel Ziegler, and Patricia Ziegler. *The Republic of Tea: Letters to a Young Zentrepreneur.* New York: Currency, 1992. A collection of pre-start-up letters between Mel and Patricia Ziegler, co-founders of Banana Republic, and Bill Rosenzweig, future founder/CEO of The Republic of Tea.

Schultz, Howard. *Pour Your Heart into It: How Starbucks Built a Company One Cup at a Time.* New York: Hyperion, 1999. Founder of Starbucks Coffee Company.

Recent Books on Mission-Driven Business

Albion, Mark. *True to Yourself: Leading a Values-Based Business.* San Francisco: Berrett-Koehler, 2006.

Arena, Christine. *Cause for Success: 10 Companies That Put Profit Second and Came in First.* Novato, CA: New World Library, 2004.

Cohen, Ben and Mal Warwick. *Values-Driven Business: How to Change the World, Make Money and Have Fun.* San Francisco: Berrett-Koehler, 2006.

Hollender, Jeffrey and Stephen Fenichell. *What Matters Most: How a Small Group of Pioneers Is Teaching Social Responsibility to Big Business, and Why Big Business Is Listening.* New York: Basic Books, 2004.

Jackson, Ira A., and Jane Nelson. *Profits with Principles.* New York: Currency, 2004.

Scott, Mary, and Howard Rothman. *Companies with a Conscience: Intimate Portraits of Twelve Firms That Make a Difference.* Radnor, PA: The Publishing Cooperative/Myers Templeton Books, 2003 (third edition).

Membership Organizations

Business Alliance for Local Living Economies (BALLE),
www.livingeconomies.org. BALLE is a North American alliance of local business networks that promote the concept of local living economies.

Co-op America Business Network (CABN), www.coopamerica.org/cabn. CABN is a network of socially and environmentally responsible businesses in the United States, and publisher of the annual National Green Pages directory.

Social Enterprise Alliance, www.se-alliance.org.
The Social Enterprise Alliance is a membership organization supporting the development of the social-enterprise sector, particularly earned-income strategies for non-profits.

Social Venture Network (SVN), www.svn.org.
SVN is a network of largely for-profit social entrepreneurs. It offers inspiration and support for current practitioners, as well as coaching and support for those just getting started.

Financial Resources

Community Development Venture Capital Alliance (CDVCA),
www.cdvca.org. CDVCA is the trade association for a subset of the venture capital industry focused on community development.

Investors' Circle, www.investorscircle.net.
Investors' Circle is a network of angel investors interested in funding mission-driven businesses. It sponsors multiple conferences, venture fairs, and retreats, annually.

Research Initiative on Social Entrepreneurship (RISE), www.riseproject.org.
RISE is a research project at the Columbia Business School whose mission is to study and disseminate knowledge about the markets, metrics, and management of for-profit and nonprofit social enterprise.

Periodicals

Fast Company, www.fastcompany.com.
A mainstream business magazine with a focus on innovation in all aspects of enterprise, including social enterprise. Publishes the annual Social Capitalist Awards.

In Business, www.jgpress.com.
A 20-year-old journal that presents case studies on small, sustainable businesses.

Stanford Social Innovation Review, www.ssireview.com.
A journal covering the social-enterprise sector, including business, non-profits, and philanthropy.

YES!, www.yesmagazine.org.
A magazine that explores a wide range of people and projects, including social enterprises, involved in creating a more "just, sustainable and compassionate world."

Index

About the Author

JILL BAMBURG is the dean of the MBA program at the Bainbridge Graduate Institute (BGI; www.bgiedu.org), a new institution offering an MBA, certificate programs, and short courses with a focus on sustainable business. She is a founding faculty member of BGI, has spearheaded the development of its unique curriculum, and has lived the lessons of getting to scale as the organization has grown from 10 students to more than 100 in four years. Her academic experience also includes seven years of teaching marketing, strategy, and general management to midcareer managers in the Graduate Management Program at Antioch University/Seattle.

Before moving into management education, Bamburg served in a variety of marketing roles at Aldus Corporation, the inventors of desktop publishing and creators of the PageMaker software program. It was at Aldus that she first became interested in questions of scale as she survived its rocket ship growth from $11 million to $180 million in revenues, from 52 employees to over 1,000, and from a single product to more than a dozen.

She is a lifelong environmentalist and spent her 20s living and working in Wyoming, including eight years of community journalism experience in Jackson Hole and a year and a half as the publisher of *High Country News*. For the last 10 years, she has served on the board of the Positive Futures Network, the publisher of *YES!* magazine.

Bamburg lives on Bainbridge Island with her daughter, Katie Gao.